Pastoral Pointers

VOLUME 2

Help for pastors faced with difficult situations

Rupert Bristow • John Cox • Paul Cox
Ed Hone • Bill Merrington • Alison Moore
John Parr • Roger Preece

Edited by John Cox

www.kevinmayhew.com

First published in Great Britain in 2014 by Kevin Mayhew Ltd
Buxhall, Stowmarket, Suffolk IP14 3BW
Tel: +44 (0) 1449 737978 Fax: +44 (0) 1449 737834
E-mail: info@kevinmayhewltd.com

www.kevinmayhew.com

9 8 7 6 5 4 3 2 1 0

ISBN 978 1 84867 697 8
Catalogue No. 1501425

Cover design by Justin Minns
© Images used under licence from Shutterstock Inc.
Edited by John Cox; copy-edited by Nicki Copeland
Typeset by Richard Weaver

Printed and bound in Great Britain

Contents

About the authors

RUPERT BRISTOW, a Reader in Trinity Benefice, Folkestone, is the author of six books of prayers and was Director of Education for Canterbury Diocese from 1995 until his retirement in 2008. He has taught on VSO, was the second Director of the UK Council for Overseas Student Affairs, and then Dean of Student Services at London South Bank University. He has also been a specialist adviser to a House of Commons Select Committee, edited and written for various educational publications and chaired Kent SACRE (Standing Advisory Council for Religious Education). He is an Honorary Fellow of Canterbury Christ Church University.

JOHN COX. Having been a parish priest in Prescot, Liverpool and Newtown, Birmingham, John spent five years as a selection secretary at Church House Westminster. He was then Director of Ordinands and Post-ordination Training for the Diocese of Southwark, and Canon of Southwark Cathedral before returning to parish life at Holy Trinity, Roehampton. In 1995 he was made Archdeacon of Sudbury and on retirement in 2006 became Diocesan Director of Education in the Diocese of St Edmundsbury and Ipswich until a second retirement in 2010. He now spends his time as Chair of Governors of a primary academy, playing golf, travelling, and writing and editing for Kevin Mayhew.

PAUL COX went into parish ministry in 1990, having been a teacher for 24 years, the last ten of which he was chaplain and headmaster of a prep school. For the next 16 years he served in rural parishes in Canterbury Diocese. At various times, he was in addition part-time Director of Selection and Training for Readers, Bishop's officer for NSMs and then OLM. On retirement to Chichester Diocese he tutors on courses for the Bishop's Certificate and is an Assistant Director of Ordinands.

ED HONE is a member of the Redemptorist missionary order and is based in Luxembourg where he is parish priest of the English-speaking Catholic community. He specialises in mission development, preaching, and creative liturgy. Currently Ed is studying for a Doctorate in Theology and Ministry at the University of Durham. He is the author of *Fit for Purpose: A Lenten Course in Spiritual Health* (2012).

BILL MERRINGTON has been an Anglican priest for more than 29 years. Originally an analytical chemist, after a serious illness he retrained in ministry and has since led churches in city, town and countryside in the West Midlands. Bill has a PhD in Psychology, specialising in the understanding of the long-term impact on parents when a child dies. He has carried out research in Britain, Lebanon, Africa and Japan, looking at the cross-cultural impact of death. He has spoken at a number of national and international conferences, and lectures regularly at universities. Bill is a qualified supervisor of counsellors and teaches regularly in counselling topics. Bill has written a number of books for both adults and children. He is currently the Lead Chaplain at Bournemouth University. Bill is married with three grown-up children.

ALISON MOORE retired at the end of 2013 as Adviser in Pastoral Care and Counselling for the Diocese of Durham, Church of England. She now does some freelance work in counselling, training and spiritual accompaniment. She is pursuing interests in music, textiles and writing, and enjoying more time with friends and family, including four grandsons. Alison was brought up in London, studied English Literature, and taught in a secondary school before moving into a career in counselling and training. She has contributed to other Kevin Mayhew publications, and believes strongly in sharing ideas in a way that is readable and accessible.

JOHN PARR is Director of Ministry, Education and Training in the Diocese of St Edmundsbury and Ipswich. He has been involved for many years in parish ministry, education and training in the Church and the voluntary sector, and has a keen interest in mental health. His work with Bible Reading Fellowship and Roots for Churches has enabled him to make biblical scholarship more widely accessible.

ROGER PREECE is vicar of Bowdon in the Diocese of Chester. With a background in business, he is a conference speaker, experienced coach and trainer in church and organisation development. He studied engineering at Imperial College and theology at Oxford University. At Oxford he was inspired by Simon Walker's work on *Undefended Leadership* and trained as a consultant in his methods. He was one of the founding managing directors of global financial solutions company Capco and led their institute for learning, research and knowledge development. Prior to that he was head of operations for an international bank. He is interested in the integration of faith and work and in the need for each individual to discover how to have a balanced life.

Introduction

John Cox

Like its predecessor, this second volume of *Pastoral Pointers* seeks to assist those who have a pastoral ministry, be it authorised or more informal, in the care of those who come to them with more unusual predicaments, seeking help either for themselves or for someone they care about.

As I wrote in the introduction to the first volume, pastoral care comes in many forms. It can be very formal and highly professionalised or more casual, such as a chat with a friend. In churches there will usually be people recognised as having a ministry of pastoral care. Most often they will have received at least some training and some form of authorisation. Many of the situations they face they will meet quite often, but there are always some that are unexpected. Of course, there are some general guidelines for pastoral care that they will be able to call on, but it is what is more specific that creates the difficulty. We cannot be experts on everything, and it does no one any good to kid people that we know everything. There may come a point when it is best to refer a person on to someone who does have the particular expertise. But between simple ignorance and specialist knowledge there is a place for informed help and caring. And this is where this book seeks to offer some help for the pastor who may well feel very anxious by their lack of even quite basic knowledge.

Each chapter offers information about a particular pastoral situation, suggestions about what help might be offered and ideas as to where further help can be found. At the beginning of the chapter there is usually a story that encapsulates some aspects of the problem. Background statistics, causes and implications are offered. While some of the help suggested may be directly applicable to the person seeking help, for the most part the advice is directed to those offering the pastoral care. The various authors have drawn upon their knowledge and their considerable experience but, in a book as brief as this, only 'pointers' can be given, not in-depth explorations and solutions. However, for most pastors this is just what is needed – pointers to indicate the general direction of things, to map out the landscape, to give some indication of what is involved and where the way forward might lie.

Abortion

Alison Moore

Story

Dan and Sue had been going out for three years. Once in the sixth form they planned to go to different universities but hoped the relationship would continue. Just as they began their A level year Sue discovered she was pregnant. Her parents were surprised, shocked and determined that this should not stand in the way of her future. 'Don't worry about it, Sue,' her mother said. 'I've made an appointment for you tomorrow. It'll soon be sorted.'

After the abortion Dan and Sue completed their degrees and married at the age of 21. Later they drifted apart, divorced amicably and each went on to second relationships. Sue had two daughters. When her elder daughter reached the sixth form, Sue found herself crying all the time, thinking about her 17-year-old self and the child she never knew. Why had her mother railroaded her into an abortion without giving her a chance to think about what she really wanted? She would never do that to her daughter.

The nature of the problem

Abortion, 'the expulsion of a foetus . . . from the womb before it is able to survive independently',[1] is an event which can occur naturally or be deliberately induced. Deliberate abortion takes place for different reasons and arouses strong and opposing views, particularly among people of faith. The very essence of what makes a human being is at stake, though people caught in a sudden shocking predicament, like Sue's mum, are unlikely to think of it like this.

Views about abortion are likely to be affected by where we live and what the legal status of abortion is there. There are many more abortions proportionately in the developing world than in developed countries, and of those, many are unsafe (i.e. carried out by someone who is unskilled in an unsuitable place). In countries which forbid or restrict abortion it becomes an unsafe procedure with potentially serious consequences for the health of the mother. Where abortion is legally permitted, it is usually safe and rates are relatively low. In the UK and USA, one in three women will have had an abortion by the time they are 45. In 2008, nearly 200,000

1. Concise Oxford English Dictionary Ninth Edition (1998).

abortions were carried out in England and Wales, and 40,000 in Scotland. Ireland has just (July 2013) legislated to allow abortion in some very limited circumstances, bringing it line with Northern Ireland's position.

The 1967 Abortion Act in the UK allows for abortion up to 24 weeks with the consent of two doctors. Although the Act stipulates that the doctors should judge that there is greater risk in continuing the pregnancy than in terminating it, in practice their decision usually goes along with 'the woman's right to choose' in matters of her own reproductive health.

Its implications

The emotional and psychological impact of abortion differs widely, of course. Like Sue, some women and men experience feelings of anxiety and guilt as well as sadness later in life about a decision for an abortion made under duress or when young. This can be compounded by the secrecy that often surrounds the event. For others, however, the sense of relief at having made the right decision is uppermost. There is no way of predicting how emotionally or psychologically damaging abortion will be.

As for the ethical implications, pro-lifers fear that the life of a new human being will be sacrificed to the superficial whim or convenience of a woman and her family. Pro-abortionists fear that the terrible pressures and oppression that women have experienced when pregnant and raising large families only increase where abortion is outlawed. Indeed, the scapegoating, punishing and blaming of pregnant women, seen in many societies throughout the world and across the ages, has been shamefully prevalent in Christian churches too. Perhaps Sue's parents wanted to avoid shame as well as help their daughter to a better future.

What might help the situation

Undoubtedly, the support, love and understanding of family and friends will help more to bring healing after a regretted decision than judgemental criticism or simplistic moral statements. If someone is considering carefully and prayerfully whether she should have an abortion because of risks to the health of the child, being told that 'of course it's wrong' (as a friend of mine was told by a vicar) is not helpful. Holding men to be as responsible for the consequences of sexual behaviour as women would help to redress the balance of blame and the culture of shame about pregnancy. In terms of supporting an individual suffering guilt, regret or shame at previous choices, liturgical structures can help someone move on once they have been thoroughly listened to and heard.

The abortion issue sharply focuses the difficulty of responding both ethically and pastorally. In rightly emotive issues like this it is good to take seriously Matthew 7:1-2:

> Do not judge, so that you may not be judged. For with the judgement you make you will be judged, and the measure you give will be the measure you get.

Ethical and pastoral responses are often different. The ethical response makes a judgement about right and wrong; the pastoral response makes no judgement but comes alongside and listens.

Agencies and sources of help

While factual information about abortion is easily accessible, it is important to be aware that the language used is very different depending on whether the organisation is 'pro-choice' or 'pro-life'. The medical and reproductive health organisations use neutral but rather chilling language: 'pregnancy termination', 'procedures' and 'abortion treatment options'. The pro-life organisations use the more emotive language of 'killing' and 'unborn child'. The websites of different organisations offer allegedly impartial factual information, but if looked at more closely the information is framed to promote their point of view.

Explore local NHS options, which should include access to counselling. If, like Sue, the abortion only surfaces as an issue years later, seek professional counselling to work through the emotions, preferably with someone who will respect any faith aspects that are important.

Scripture and prayer

At the heart of its story, Christianity remembers a young unmarried mother who, surprisingly, was not taken for a back-street abortion but undoubtedly suffered for the shame of her condition. Christianity also has a history of caring for those who are vulnerable, rejected or condemned for choices they have made. And the gospel is good news of hope and forgiveness, of new life for any who turn to Christ, with the promise of leaving behind the 'old life' and taking on the new.

> So if anyone is in Christ, there is a new creation: everything old has passed away; see, everything has become new!
>
> *2 Corinthians 5:17*

Oh God, Lord of life, the conqueror of death, our help in time of trouble,
you do not willingly grieve or afflict your children.
Strengthen those who mourn, cleanse those who are afflicted by shame or guilt;
give us grace, in the presence of death and in memory of the lives that could never be lived,
to worship you, that we may have sure hope with them of eternal life,
and put our whole trust in your goodness and mercy;
through Jesus Christ our Lord,
Amen.

Birth control

Alison Moore

Story

The school nurse gave her usual talk to the teenagers about sexual health and relationships, including a description of the different contraceptives that were available. Gemma was relieved she didn't have to ask anything – she'd felt really stupid when her boyfriend had said, 'You are on the pill, aren't you?' She hadn't wanted to admit that she wasn't and she had been too embarrassed to ask him to wear a condom. She made herself an appointment with the GP, who was a matter-of-fact woman who made her feel like an adult and simply sorted it out for her.

Later Gemma's mother found the evidence at home, and that was when the family trouble started. Her mother was really into going to Mass – in fact, she went every day. She told Gemma that she was doubly sinful – for sleeping with her boyfriend and for taking the pill, which 'killed babies'.

The nature of the problem

Birth control, in the form of safe, effective and cheap contraception, is a relatively new phenomenon, but in our society it is now generally accepted as a normal part of life, as uncontentious as headache pills. Contraception involves blocking either conception itself or the very earliest stages of the foetus in the womb. Many different methods can be used, natural or artificial, including abstinence from intercourse, adjusting sexual activity in line with a woman's fertility cycle, using physical objects to prevent insemination, using chemical or herbal compounds or taking hormonal substances to prevent pregnancy developing.

Birth control is perhaps not likely to present itself as a 'problem' in pastoral encounters, as couples are likely to use some form of birth control regardless of their religious background. This applies even to people who are faithful to the Roman Catholic Church, which holds a clear position that artificial contraception is wrong because it stops a marriage being open to the possibility of new life. However, it may present as a problem if it involves teenagers, as in Gemma's case, if it has not worked, if there is disagreement over the right kind of birth control, or when different generations hold differing views.

Its implications

Because contraception is so much a part of ordinary life, the pastor may not pick up cues that someone is experiencing difficulties with issues to do with what it means for them and how it is affecting their life and relationships. It is worth remembering that when discussing birth control, potentially powerful, though not necessarily visible, factors will be present, stemming from family, social, educational, economic and religious backgrounds.

Contraception raises issues of whose right it is to decide whether to have children and whose right it is to choose to enjoy sex without the possibility of pregnancy. Pastoral issues may arise when men have been denied a role in the birth control decision, or when parents have not been allowed to know what their children, particularly daughters, have been choosing. Parents can find it difficult to face up to the reality that their children are becoming sexually active. Strong emotional forces can be at play in a family as parents watch their daughter becoming a woman and their son changing through puberty. For parents, the contrast with their own ageing and changing sex drive can be stark, and the contraception issue can be muddled up in that.

What might help

The pastoral carer needs to be aware of the possibility of strong emotions in a family if the contraception issue is to do with teenagers. There may be feelings of anger and powerlessness if health professionals have given contraception to underage girls without the parents' knowledge. Take seriously whatever is described – what may seem to you to be overreactions or unnecessary anxieties may be masking real fears, guilt or sadness. Take care if one member of a family or couple has confided in you, as this can lead to complexities of confidentiality. You may find yourself agreeing with opinions, holding secrets or betraying confidences in ways you don't really want to. If Gemma were to speak with you, you might be able to help her explore what she really wants in her relationship with her boyfriend, including sexually. And although you may feel sympathetic to or critical of her mother's beliefs or behaviour, you would need to maintain a neutral position that respects her mother.

Agencies and sources of help

For factual or medical information:

GP surgery: Your local surgery will have written information, and a conversation with your doctor or practice nurse would answer practical questions.

NHS website: www.nhs.uk[2] Here you will find a full section of information and questions answered:

http://www.nhs.uk/Conditions/contraception-guide/Pages/contraception.aspx[3]

For relationship counselling:

Relate: www.relate.org.uk[4]
Marriage Care: www.marriagecare.org.uk[5]

Prayer

Lord God,
thank you for the mystery and wonder of conception;
thank you for the joy and beauty of sexual relationships;
thank you for the variety of ways in which the natural world renews and limits itself.
We pray for those who are making choices about children:
for those who bear the pain of not being able to have children,
for those who need to make a decision about not having children.
We pray for wisdom and responsibility,
for trust in your unsearchable and fathomless love,
even when we get things wrong or make choices we regret.
In Jesus' name.
Amen.

---

2. Accessed 22 November 2013.
3. Accessed 22 November 2013.
4. Accessed 22 November 2013.
5. Accessed 22 November 2013.

Cancer

Rupert Bristow

Story

Stories about cancer sufferers can take many forms: miraculous recovery, swift decline and death, early surgery and ongoing chemo- or radiotherapy. The one thing that is common to all such stories is that each case is unique, just as each person is special, both in the eyes of the person and their loved ones – and in the sight of God. There is therefore a natural reticence for people to tell their own stories, as those who have recovered know that 'but for the grace of God . . .' and those who are not expected to recover rarely want to share their story of terminal decline. Of course, even in the latter case, there may be relatives who after their loved one's death want to speak about the courage and selflessness of the cancer sufferer, especially where there is a high-profile story that is traced in the media or where the person raises huge sums against all odds in a feat of cycling, walking, sailing or swimming.

The purpose of a story is to know where that journey has started, where it has led, where it is now – and where it may lead. No extended family or close-knit community is free from stories about cancer, be they lung cancer (now not so frequent, mercifully), breast cancer (high profile and with a high recovery rate if diagnosed in time), child leukaemia (heart-rending), cervical cancer (for which a preventive vaccination is being widely used) or the male preserves of prostate and testicular cancers.

A story to illustrate not the illness but the state of mind that can be induced, one way or the other, during treatment was the jockey Bob Champion's account of his experience when he was at his lowest during his treatment for testicular cancer. He said that when he was wondering whether he could take the treatment any more, he walked out of his ward and found himself by the children's ward, where there were children with cancers who seemed to just be getting on with it. At that moment he decided that if they could cope, then so should he.

Statistics

Around 300,000 new cases of cancer are diagnosed each year in the UK. More than one in three people will develop some form of cancer in their lifetime. Between 1978 and 2007, incidence rates for cancer in Great Britain increased by 25 per cent, with a four per cent increase in men and a 32 per cent increase in women. In the last decade incidence rates have remained fairly constant. There are more than 200 different types of cancer, but four of them – breast, lung, large bowel and prostate – account for over half (54 per cent) of new cases.

Causes

Many will blame modern lifestyles and diet for some of the causes of cancer, just as the decline in smoking has undeniably reduced the incidence of lung cancer. However, with the increase in life expectancy comes a greater risk that some form of cancer may be the final cause of death after a long and full life. The view is changing from its being primarily a disease that strikes people in the prime of life.

Help

Being there for the cancer sufferer is one of the few common features of both practical and pastoral help. That may mean talking; it may require a lot of listening; it may mean both praying with and praying for the person. Christian hope can be a great help to both recovering cancer sufferers and those who find they have a terminal illness. But there may well be rage at times – at God, at the health service, at family or friends who don't communicate or who just get it wrong in trying to be sensitive and ending up being anything but.

Church communities usually contain an amazing mix of backgrounds, skills and qualities. Help can vary from meals offered to the sufferer and/or family at crucial times, to praying with the person, to looking after the household pet, to offering transportation on treatment days, to being a sounding board for next steps, to keeping the garden in trim. A church that cannot muster this kind of support is simply failing the test of a community which purports to care.

There will always be differing approaches to prayers for healing or miracle cures, but we must believe that the medical skills and research endeavours of individuals and hospitals are God given and are part of God's creation, so using what is on offer seems Christian common sense. The services in each area will vary, but in addition to the cancer care services of the NHS in hospitals are the invaluable support of Macmillan nurses, the network of hospices for both terminal and respite care, mostly funded by voluntary efforts, along with GP practices and private provision.

Despite recent threats to cut them back, chaplaincy services really come into their own in caring for those who have lengthy stays in hospital. Chaplaincy teams are often multi-faith but with a strong ecumenical Christian element, and a tip-off to the chaplain usually results in an early visit or the offer of communion.

Churches will also have very different approaches to pastoral visiting and pastoral care, from very sophisticated arrangements and procedures, which may sometimes depend too much on a few individuals or an overly mechanistic approach, to a vague 'better tell the vicar' policy, which inevitably leads to overload. Healing services or slots for healing ministry during or after a service are on the increase in many churches and are much more of a mainstream ministry, following the example of Jesus and his disciples, than in the recent past. Building up good practice and giving appropriate training and authorisation in these areas can help equip people to meet at least some of the challenges that cancer sufferers, members of their families, neighbours and other members of the congregation may experience.

Past sufferers will have a special empathy, but should beware reliving their disease with current sufferers who may not cope with that approach. Sharing experiences when asked can be helpful if sensitivity is shown to the sufferer's needs – and we should remember that a 'cancer survivor' always lives with an underlying fear of the disease returning.

Prayers

Healing Lord,
let nature and the skills of doctors
join forces to mend and tend
all afflicted with cancer.
Let diagnosis be quick and treatment timely,
and may the knowledge of your presence
be a comfort and a shield,
to patient and carer alike.
Amen.

God of the personal,
help us never to make assumptions about people's illness
or the treatment they receive.
May every step of recovery from cancer
be blessed with understanding and thanks,
and every setback be accompanied
by renewed prayer and encouragement.
May we combine the cure of disease with the cure of souls.
Amen.

Lord of healing and wholeness,
we pray for those recovering from cancer
and those whose treatment is just beginning.
As each person is different and distinct,
so each illness is personal and individual.
May we show our empathy,
not only in our words and wishes,
but also in our practical assistance,
those little unremembered acts
of kindness, love and friendship.
Amen.

(From *Prayers for Inclusion and Diversity* by Rupert Bristow, Kevin Mayhew, 2012)

Childlessness

John Parr

Story

Annie has always enjoyed the company of children. During her last year at school she volunteered at a local nursery. After university she worked as a nanny for nine months while she decided what she wanted to do next. At weddings and family gatherings she would always spend time with the children. She gave everyone the impression that once she was settled, she would soon have children of her own.

Annie and Andy have been together for ten years. They are happy in their relationship and successful in their respective careers, so much so that they live comfortably and, by their own admission, 'want for nothing'. They have no children, and until recently they took in their stride the gentle enquiries of their more sensitive family members and friends about their 'plans for the future', and even the more forthright comments of those who insisted on reminding them of the relentless ticking of the biological clock and the perils of having teenagers as a fifty-something.

Two years ago Andy was involved in a serious car accident. He made a good recovery, but the accident made them both think about the future, and particularly children. They realised that they'd allowed the hopes that they'd both had for a family when they first met to recede. Their demanding jobs had brought the material rewards that they'd come to take for granted. Now in their mid-thirties, they felt that Andy's accident had rekindled their earlier hopes, and they began to imagine themselves as parents.

For the first year, imagination was about as far as they went. They were surprised how anxious they became, because they'd always seen themselves as easy-going and unruffled. After another six months, one of Andy's work colleagues was about to begin maternity leave, and he was taken aback by the mixture of envy and irritation he felt. Then out of the blue an old school friend got in touch with Annie; they hadn't seen each other for years. Kate was keen to share the news that she was expecting her third child. 'We never really thought much about having children,' she remarked casually. 'They just seem to happen.' Kate's unthinking bluntness – something Annie recalled as one of her enduring characteristics – raised all kinds of 'what ifs' in Annie's mind.

'What if there's something wrong with one of us? What if the accident has affected things? What if we've left it too late?' These were the questions Annie put to Andy after Kate's visit. They both realised how much of their customary composure they'd started to lose.

Some statistics

In England and Wales, one in five women born in 1965 is childless (for statistical purposes, this is defined as having no children by the age of 46). This compares with one in nine women born in 1938.[6] The figures are similar in the USA,[7] and higher in Germany (28 per cent).[8]

In England and Wales, the second most common family size for the 1965 cohort is to be childless (the most common is two children). This was the least common family size for women born between 1930 and 1945.[9]

The peak age range for giving birth is 30–34. IVF has a 30 per cent success rate among women in their late twenties and early thirties. This falls to 5 per cent for women aged 44 using their own eggs.[10]

Attitudes related to childlessness

- There is evidence that as governments introduce more child- and family-friendly policies, such as maternity/paternity leave, part-time working and family tax credits, childless people become more resentful at having to make sacrifices to support families with children. These include paying more taxes and covering for parents taking statutory employment leave.
- Working women with children may be seen as being less committed to their jobs.
- Families with a higher number of children may be regarded as environmentally irresponsible.
- Though it is now more socially acceptable for people to be childless, some couples with children see those who choose to be without children as self-absorbed or materialistic.

6. Office for National Statistics: 'Cohort Fertility, England and Wales 2011', available at http://www.ons.gov.uk/ons/dcp171778_299058.pdf (accessed 22 November 2013).
7. See http://www.census.gov/hhes/fertility/data/cps/2010.html (accessed 22 November 2013).
8. Toshihiko Hara (2008), 'Increasing Childlessness in Germany and Japan: Towards a Childless Society?' in *The International Journal of Japanese Sociology*, 17:42-62; available at http://onlinelibrary.wiley.com/doi/10.1111/j.1475-6781.2008.00110.x/full (accessed 22 November 2013).
9. Office for National Statistics: 'Cohort Fertility, England and Wales 2011'.
10. Office for National Statistics: 'Cohort Fertility, England and Wales 2011'.

Taken together, these attitudes suggest that couples with children and couples without children may regard each other as a different species, with each claiming to occupy the moral high ground.

Why childlessness is increasing in the developed world

Research suggests a number of reasons:

- The proportion of people who are married or in stable relationships is declining.
- The economic value of children has declined with the ending of child labour and the development of social care. At the same time, the financial implications of having children are rising, as children take on the role of consumers from an early age and take ever longer to outgrow financial dependency on their parents.
- Mothers experience significant role conflicts between their workplace and domestic roles in societies where traditional role expectations remain strong, or where support for working mothers is inadequate or expensive.
- There are changes in the perceived benefits and costs of childrearing compared to pursuing a career, which allows people the freedom to aspire to a higher standard of living.
- The increasing availability of safe, effective contraception has enabled women to choose whether to become mothers rather than having motherhood imposed on them.
- It is now more socially acceptable for people to be childless.
- Postponing the decision to have children increases the risk of involuntary childlessness among women, as it may then be biologically too late to conceive and give birth.
- Research from Germany shows correlations between childlessness and participation in higher education, urbanisation, declining religious activity, women's involvement in full-time employment and low income. Of unmarried, highly educated women in full-time employment, 89 per cent are childless. The figure falls to 65 per cent among women with no higher education, who prefer a consumer lifestyle to having children.[11]

Commentators suggest that post-modern societies are marked by increasing competition between the inherited models of couple and family formation, and the pursuit of individual freedom. We may be seeing the emergence of a culture of childlessness, where men and women increasingly find their identity by choosing their own values and associated lifestyles. They make choices as to whether to form a

---

11. Hara, 'Increasing Childlessness in Germany and Japan: Towards a Childless Society?', p.51.

couple, with the ever higher expectations this brings, or to remain single; whether to have a family, with the related decisions about the particular shape of parental roles, or to remain childless; whether to pursue or to sacrifice career and lifestyle aspirations. Where once parenthood was seen as an expression of human fulfilment, it is now more commonly seen as an obstacle.

Informing the pastoral response

The key issue is what the childless person or couple represent. For some it will be the frustrated desire to have a child. There may be reproductive problems that can be fixed in one way or another, or it may be impossible, or even too late. The wise pastor will be alert to a range of feelings, from heartache to guilt, and the most appropriate ways of helping. For other couples who are happy or resigned to being childless, the frustrations may arise from the behaviour or attitudes of those in their world who are parents, or those in their circle who see parenthood as natural and normative. Here, pastoral wisdom will seek to reassure and sustain those who do not seek to be other than they are.

The Bible can exacerbate the frustration and pain of those who do not choose to be childless. The Genesis mandate to 'be fruitful and multiply' may be taken to suggest that marriage and its contemporary equivalents are incomplete without children (see Genesis 1:28; 9:1, 7). Attitudes like this are particularly strong when it is believed that the primary (or, indeed, the sole) purpose of sexual intercourse is procreation. Childlessness may simply be seen as failure. And in societies where childbearing is essential for survival, or viewed as a gift from God, childlessness is regarded as shameful – a sign of divine judgement that is borne especially by women. This is how the biblical world tends to view childlessness. Women such as Sarai (Genesis 15:2; 16:1), Hannah (1 Samuel 1) and Elizabeth (Luke 1:7) are stigmatised as barren. There is no suggestion that they and their husbands are simply childless, which would allow either the man or the woman to be considered as infertile. In each of their stories, divine intervention remedies what is essentially a female problem.

But the Bible also offers an alternative approach. Jesus' words to the women of Jerusalem on the Via Dolorosa open up the possibility of seeing childlessness as a blessed rather than a cursed condition (Luke 23:29). This is in line with his challenge to the gender and family stereotypes of his day, whereby women find their highest calling as wives and mothers, and blood-related families form the foundations of God's people (Luke 8:1-3, 19-21; 11:27). Jesus' critique of the traditional wisdom of his world calls us to be similarly vigilant towards attitudes and behaviours in our own, shaped as they are by convention or consumer choice. And it provides comfort and reassurance for those who are childless, whether by choice or not.

Sources of help

For information about the causes of infertility and the treatment that is available in the UK, see www.nhs.uk/Conditions/Infertility/Pages/Introduction.aspx[12]

Infertility Network UK is a national charity providing support, information and advice to those who are struggling to conceive: www.infertilitynetworkuk.com[13]

ACeBabes provides information, support and advice to the growing number of people successfully using fertility treatment, surrogacy, adoption or fostering to become parents: www.infertilitynetworkuk.com/ace_babes[14]

More to Life! provides information and support for those who are involuntarily childless: www.infertilitynetworkuk.com/moretolife/[15]

COTS (Childlessness Overcome Through Surrogacy UK) is a voluntary surrogacy organisation working through the UK. It provides information to surrogates and would-be parents, helping them to understand the implications of surrogacy before they enter into an arrangement and to deal with any problems that may arise during it: www.surrogacy.org.uk.[16]

Prayer

God our creator,
you make all people in your image
and call us to serve you whatever our condition.
Give us wisdom to use our gifts and capabilities
responsibly, wisely and for the good of the wider world.
When our longings and aspirations are frustrated or impeded,
open our hearts to find new strength and hope
and enlarge our vision to see new possibilities for our lives.
Amen.

---

12. Accessed 23 November 2013.
13. Accessed 23 November 2013.
14. Accessed 23 November 2013.
15. Accessed 23 November 2013.
16. Accessed 23 November 2013.

Corruption in the workplace

Roger Preece

What is it?

Not many of us have had an experience similar to that of Mike Woodward, who arrived in his dream job as president and chief executive of Olympus, the Japanese camera maker, to discover that three companies worth very little had been bought for $1.7 billion. He questioned the board and asked for an explanation. When none came, he commissioned his own investigation into the matter and was promptly fired. It was later proved that the deals were fraudulent and were designed to cover up previous losses. Although he was eventually compensated, Woodward risked everything by challenging the board of his company.

Or what of the senior banking executives who all signed up to bundling payment protection insurance (PPI) along with loans offered to customers. The customers were charged extra for this insurance, which turned out to be practically useless to most people. The subsequent scandal was estimated at the end of 2013 to cost Britain's banks around £18 billion.[17] Who made the decision to force customers to buy a product that they wouldn't need, and why did all the banks join in, even banks that prided themselves on their ethical standards such as the Co-operative Bank? Thousands of bankers involved with this scandal must have wondered if it was OK, but almost no one was willing to blow the whistle.

The pressures in business are considerable. Meeting targets, acquiring customers, maximising revenue from customers, driving up profits are all important parts of business life. But if they are carried out without a good ethical framework, they can lead at best to taking advantage of customers and, at worst, to criminal fraud and corruption. At a meeting on 5 September 2012, Martin Wheatley, CEO of the Financial Conduct Authority, the body responsible for financial conduct in the UK, said he was giving banks time to 'get their houses in order, for example by voluntarily winding down the flawed incentive schemes that can encourage retail banking staff to sweet-talk, hoodwink or bully ill-informed customers into taking out often worthless and over-priced financial products.'[18]

---

17. www.risk.net (accessed 17 December 2013).
18. As reported by Ian Fraser, www.ianfraser.org/martin-wheatley-how-bank-staff-are-encouraged-to-mis-sell/, 7 September 2012 (accessed 17 December 2013).

Most of us can see the clear rights and wrongs of the Olympus scandal, but can we be sure that we would have been willing to complain to our management about the PPI products that were so profitable at the time? And what of the more straightforward issues of cheating on expense claims? Most people who cheat generally have a logical reason for why their claim is justified. The UK MPs who were found to have cheated on their claims in the expense scandal all offered arguments to attempt to justify their behaviour, to make it acceptable within their own ethics.

What are the impacts?

Pastoral support may be requested in different scenarios:

Someone who has clearly identified corruption in the workplace and is anxious about what to do about it and what might be the consequences

- Confidential advice and support will be necessary.
- The consequences of raising a complaint need to be considered.
- The person's motivations also need to be understood, as well as the level of risk of acting or of failing to act. There may be moral dilemmas that need to be weighed up. For example, a manager may be acting wrongly, but the company may be destroyed and everyone lose their jobs if the wrongdoing is made public. Is the claim valid and is the person who suspects a problem sure of their facts?
- The temptation to do nothing and avoid the issues will be strong.
- If they decide to raise the matter, the individual may be subject to harassment, intimidation, isolation or other threats. They may lose their job. There are legal safeguards in place to protect those who make disclosures in the public interest. A trade union or employment lawyer may need to be consulted.

Someone who has a business responsibility and is concerned about the ethics of their actions or their company's policies

- Expert, confidential and supportive advice will be needed.
- Peer networks and organisations dedicated to improving business standards will be of help.
- There will be a need for assistance in seeing the long-term impact on professional standing and business success versus the desire for a short-term 'fix'.

Someone who has been found guilty of corruption and is struggling to get their life back in order

- For someone who has been fired or disciplined at work for corruption, the path of recovery is hard. It will likely have been a public disgrace with all the consequent damaging of personal reputation.

- The individual may need help reflecting on what happened and how they got into the mess that led to such disaster. They may feel that they have been unfairly treated, or even that they have been made a scapegoat. In-depth pastoral prayer, and perhaps counselling, may be helpful to get to the root causes of what went wrong.
- Repentance, receiving forgiveness and a determination to turn around are elements of the spiritual journey that will be part of the normal offering of pastoral care.
- In addition, being able to link up with a small group of peers in the business world for personal support and encouragement will be important. Having a small group of friends around will be essential.
- The individual may need support in connecting with people in different walks of life, where past failures would not be a barrier to entry. This could involve career coaching.
- The church can help the recovery process by being willing to give the individual appropriate responsibility in the church or related charities that could help the individual rebuild their confidence and reputation. However, certain conditions would bar someone from being a trustee under charity law, e.g. those with unspent convictions, bankrupts or under an 'individual voluntary arrangement' to deal with debts or if they have been disqualified as a company director.[19]

Resources

For the whistle blower

- Public Concern at Work: this is a registered charity that advises individuals and businesses in dealing with complaints about practices that are identified by insiders: www.pcaw.org.uk[20]
- WikiLeaks: publisher of confidential information that they think should be in the public domain. Gives examples of potentially corrupt practices in different parts of the world. www.wikileaks.org[21]

For the business leader

Pastorally, it is more likely that discussions with business leaders regarding corruption are going to be related to morally grey areas

19. See the Charity Commission for details: www.charitycommission.gov.uk (accessed 17 December 2013).
20. Accessed 24 November 2013.
21. Accessed 24 November 2013.

that border between unethical and corrupt behaviours. Someone who is criminally intent on corruption is unlikely to come for pastoral conversations.

- The Institute for Business Ethics, an independent charity founded in 1986 that originated from the Christian Association of Business Executives. They provide a range of reports, workshops and training for all who are concerned with the ethics of the workplace. www.ibe.org.uk[22]
- Centre for Business and Public Sector Ethics, Cambridge. Founded in 1988, the organisation provides research and reports into ethical issues for business. www.ethicscentre.org[23]
- Faith in Business at Ridley Hall Cambridge. Centre for research and development of Christian practice in the workplace. Their annual conference attracts senior-level speakers with insights into good business practices in the competitive workplace. www.ridley.cam.ac.uk/centres/faith-in-business[24]

For the fallen executive

- Spiritual direction – working with a trained spiritual director is valuable for all Christians, especially those needing to recover and to find restoration. The right help may come from a referral by a local church or diocese, or you could consider The London Centre for Spirituality which has resources and access to directories of trained Directors.

Retreat in a supportive community:

- Scargill House: www.scargillmovement.org[25]
- The community of Aidan and Hilda on Lindisfarne: www.aidanandhilda.org.uk[26]
- L'Abri community: http://www.labri.org/england/index.html[27]
- Lee Abbey in Devon: www.leeabbey.org.uk[28]

These are some examples of communities that offer retreat programmes or allow space for personal visits in a supportive environment.

22. Accessed 24 November 2013.
23. Accessed 24 November 2013.
24. Accessed 24 November 2013.
25. Accessed 24 November 2013.
26. Accessed 24 November 2013.
27. Accessed 24 November 2013.
28. Accessed 24 November 2013.

Scripture and meditation

> Can I forget the treasures of wickedness in the house of the wicked, and the scant measure that is accursed? Can I tolerate wicked scales and a bag of dishonest weights?
>
> *Micah 6:10-11*

The Old and New Testaments have many words to say about honesty and justice. There is a special emphasis on the rich and powerful not abusing their position with respect to the poor. Christians should go out of their way not just to be honest but also to have a reputation for honesty.

Paul writes to Timothy, urging that leaders be above reproach and has much wisdom for the character of a leader (see 1 Timothy 3). This suggests that they live their lives in a way that seeks to avoid moral ambiguity and are known to be people of integrity and honour. This is a high calling, and we need all the help and advice we can get.

Prayer

God of honour and integrity,
bless all those involved with business and commerce.
May they be faithful in small things that you may entrust them with much.
May those in power never take unfair advantage of their position.
May those who discover injustice have the courage to speak out,
that your will may be done on Earth as it is in heaven.
Amen.

Cults

Ed Hone

Dangerous territory

In 1978 the attention of the world was focused on 'Jonestown', the Guyana headquarters of the Peoples Temple Agricultural Project, a movement founded by Jim Jones. Jonestown hit the headlines when more than 900 members of the group died as a result of cyanide poisoning at the bidding of Jones. What could influence so many people to take such drastic action? What dynamic was at work? Jonestown represents, in a spectacular fashion, the dangers associated with cults: how ordinary men and women can be manipulated into behaving in extraordinary ways, sometimes with tragic results.

There are no clear, unambiguous definitions of what constitutes a cult (sometimes referred to as a 'new religious movement'), but there are generally agreed characteristics. The founder of a cult is usually a charismatic individual with exceptional powers of persuasion or manipulation: they are able to convince others to join them in their beliefs and lifestyle, even when such action seems irrational and countercultural. Cult members define themselves as set apart, elite in some way, and usually live in a controlled environment with minimal unrestricted contact with the world outside. This often means that they operate according to their own internal moral code, where right and wrong are defined by the cult itself. And whereas the rhetoric of the cult is often idealistic, there is seldom any contribution to wider society: the objective is simply the perpetuation of the cult and its membership.

Who joins a cult?

It is tempting to imagine that cult members are necessarily gullible, uneducated and from less well-off backgrounds; this is not usually the case, however. Rather, people who join cults are more often than not generally well educated, idealistic and from comfortable backgrounds.

What threat do cults pose? Once involved in a cult it can be difficult, if not impossible, to leave. Psychological manipulation, erosion of one's own free will and emotional blackmail all reduce the capacity for independent action and make members vulnerable. Separation from family and friends increases dependence on the cult, to the point where life outside becomes virtually unimaginable; the leader may warn of the evil intentions of non-members in trying to lure members away, and paranoia feeds paranoia.

What can the Christian do to help someone who wishes to escape a cult?

What advice can we give to those who are anxious about a loved one who belongs to a cult? The first step is to find out as much information as possible about the organisation concerned: is it really a cult? Are its members free to leave? Is it harming its members? There are numerous organisations and information sites offering advice and help – some of these are listed below. These organisations have often been founded by former cult members, and they offer wise advice.

Secondly, encourage the person to maintain as much contact as possible with the person for whom they are concerned, without coercing them. Then watch out for any characteristics of the cult that are overtly harmful or illegal. Keeping a log of conversations, actions, concerns and contact can be useful in giving an overview of what has happened, and of any worrying trends that might be developing. It is good to avoid ridiculing or criticising the cult as this may reinforce a siege mentality and cause the member to withdraw from further contact. A non-judgemental, accepting attitude is more likely to help keep the lines of communication open.

Support is needed not only for members of cults wishing to escape, but also for families and loved ones. Because of the psychological implications of cult membership, it is important for the pastor to seek the best advice and to refer those in need of help to qualified practitioners (e.g. counsellors, therapists, etc.) as and when appropriate.

The words of Jeannie Mills, a victim of the Jonestown tragedy, are worth noting:

> When you meet the friendliest people you have ever known, who introduce you to the most loving group of people you've ever encountered, and you find the leader to be the most inspired, caring, compassionate and understanding person you've ever met, and then you learn the cause of the group is something you never dared hope could be accomplished, and all of this sounds too good to be true – it probably is too good to be true! Don't give up your education, your hopes and ambitions to follow a rainbow.

Organisations

- Spotlight Ministries – a Christian-based organisation. The site lists ten marks of a cult and gives pointers to responding to cult members in a supportive way. The site also includes a useful list of 'Dos and Don'ts': http://www.spotlightministries.org.uk/clt.htm[29]
- Cult Information Centre – offers a clear overview of issues pertaining to cults, along with resources for discovering more and acting effectively: http://www.cultinformation.org.uk/[30]
- Inform – The Information Network on Religious Movements – links to a variety of general and specific self-help groups internationally: http://www.inform.ac/other-organisations-offering-support[31]

Scripture

We are set free by the word of God

> Then Jesus said to the Jews who had believed in him, 'If you continue in my word, you are truly my disciples; and you will know the truth, and the truth will make you free.'
>
> *John 8:31-32*

Prayer

Heavenly Father,
help us to live by the word of your Son, Jesus Christ.
His word is a word of life,
a liberating word.
Living by his word,
we will be true disciples,
becoming more like our master,
drawn more into the life of God.
May we know your truth, and be truly free.
Amen.

29. Accessed 24 November 2013.
30. Accessed 24 November 2013.
31. Accessed 24 November 2013.

Debt

Roger Preece

What is it?

Few of us can live in the modern world without the use of debt. Whether it be the use of a credit card, a car loan, a mortgage or the occasional dipping into an overdraft with our banks, the use of debt is now very normal. The introduction of student loans and full fees of £9000 per year for many university courses in 2012 means that, including living expenses, many students will walk into the world of work with a debt of £50,000 hanging around their necks.

According to the Bank of England, at the end of October 2013, outstanding consumer debt was around £158 billion.[32] At 20 per cent interest, this would generate around £86,000,000 per day in interest charges to be paid to financial institutions.

What are the impacts?

One of the changes in society over the last 30 years is the ease with which consumer debt can be obtained and the way in which having large debts is considered to be a normal part of life. The development of student loans will increase the acceptance of high levels of indebtedness. For a young adult who is expected to have a large debt from their student loan, an additional £20,000 may not seem too great a burden, although the interest rate on a personal loan can be crippling.

The rise of pay-day loans and the aggressive advertising linked to them is creating a new generation of people trapped in a downward spiral of higher payments to meet debts that increase as interest rolls up. Firms such as Wonga, one of the fastest-growing of the new companies, publicly advertise eye-watering levels of interest for short-term borrowing – in excess of 5000 per cent. The UK government has announced that it intends to regulate this business following a cross-party review of the industry.[33] Even the Archbishop of Canterbury, Justin Welby, entered the debate with his suggestion that the churches should work to find alternative sources of short-term lending to compete with the pay-day loan companies.[34] The problems with this business include aggressive advertising that creates a demand, and incredible ease of use: within a few clicks on

32. Bank of England – Statistical Release – Money and Credit, published 29 November 2013.
33. As reported on BBC Today programme, 25 November 2013.
34. As reported in the *Independent*, 25 July 2013.

a website, money can be in someone's account and a direct debit authorised that allows the lender to take money out of the borrower's bank account without any thought to their real needs.

In helping people to think about debt, there needs to be a distinction between debts that can be beneficial and those that are effectively a waste of money. When interest rates are low and fixed, it can make good sense to borrow money to allow income to increase or to obtain an asset that will rise in value. However, in a housing market in which prices are falling, it would be a disastrous time to take out a large mortgage. It would be better to rent and then buy later when prices are lower. A decision to enter into a mortgage is often taken emotionally – i.e. wanting to fulfil the desire to own one's own home – yet the reality is that the bank owns the rights to the home, and you are paying them rent on the money they have advanced until every penny is paid back! In a rising housing market, borrowing to buy a property can be a fantastic investment, but many people aren't able to separate the rational investment risk/reward action from the desire to own their own bricks and mortar.

We need to take the emotion out of the decision to borrow money and help people to consider the overall costs and the risks of getting tied in to long-term debt.

What can be done?

When consumer credit first became widely available with the launch of credit cards, the advertising slogan for Access, a precursor to the Mastercard brand, was 'Take the waiting out of wanting'. This is at the heart of indebtedness. The desire is to consume now and worry about paying later, as distinct from a culture of saving now so I can enjoy later without the extra costs. The power of advertising to seduce us with high premium brands is another factor in creating unnecessary debt. A generic tablet computer will provide all the same functions as an iPad yet at one-third of the price, yet people on low incomes will often extend themselves to buy the more highly valued brand even though it is not necessary.

Pastorally we need to help people understand the dangers of debt and be willing to consider putting the waiting back into acquiring. Young people need to be given opportunities to become financially literate. They need to be able to distinguish between cheap financing and expensive borrowing and to realise that even so-called 'free credit' is never truly free, as the costs of the credit will be included in the product, meaning that a discount is probably possible by negotiation.

Learning to be content with what we have and with spending within our means is the first principle in resisting unnecessary debt. Learning to save up to acquire the things we need will help us to avoid debt. Being able to sell things we no longer need will help improve our finances. Organisations such as eBay can be a great help in this respect. Learning how to budget will help us to know what surplus income we have that can help us to pay off debt in the future if we do need to borrow. Financial literacy will help us to obtain the cheapest forms of debt when we need to borrow for good reasons.

If people find themselves in serious debt that is out of control and they do not have the income to pay the interest charges, they must obtain help quickly. One of the challenges is that some of the so-called debt management services themselves are unethical. They can end up charging high fees to clients, who end up in a worse state. Some debt websites are nothing more than marketing collecting points for gathering possible clients. They are then bundled up and sold on to other agencies.

Organisations such as The Money Charity (formerly Credit Action), the Citizens Advice Bureau, and the National Debtline can all provide assistance and point to good places for help.

There are ways of dealing with excessive debt, but they are complicated and all need specialist help. They include:

- *Debt management plans* – which involve agreeing new payment terms and reduced interest rates with creditors
- *Bankruptcy* – which wipes out debts but has very serious long-term consequences
- *Individual Voluntary Agreement* (IVA) – which allows reduced payments calculated out of surplus monthly income from a basic budget
- *Debt Relief Order* (DRO) – for smaller amounts when you have a very low income.

Resources

- Christians against Poverty (CAP) – debt counselling, debt management, personal budget coaching and training in financial management. In 2012 CAP managed over £42,000,000 of debt for clients: www.capuk.org[35]
- The Money Charity (formerly Credit Action) – provides data, education resources and tools to help with debt management: www.themoneycharity.org.uk[36]

35. Accessed 24 November 2013.
36. Accessed 24 November 2013.

- Citizens Advice Bureau: www.citizensadvice.org.uk[37]
- Step Change – offers free expert advice on debt management solutions: www.stepchange.org[38]
- *The Money Secret* by Rob Parsons (Hodder and Stoughton, 2005) – practical wisdom on how to stay debt free and how to get out of debt.
- *Handling Money God's Way* by Keith Tondeur (New Wine Publications, 2001) – excellent booklet on good principles for financial management and stewardship.
- *The Sixty Minute Debt Buster* by Katie Clarke with Rob Parsons (Lion Hudson, 2009) – very practical and clearly written guide on dealing with debt.
- *The Money Revolution* by John Preston (Authentic Media, 2007) – this is a general book to help people to develop a sensible attitude to money, which can help avoid the problems of bad debt.

Scripture

> But godliness with contentment is great gain. For we brought nothing into the world, and we can take nothing out of it. But if we have food and clothing, we will be content with that.
>
> *1 Timothy 6:6-8 (NIV UK)*

We all need to develop contentment with what we have. We all need an ability to still the inner voice of discontent that is fuelled by advertising. Advertising typically tries to persuade us that happiness, beauty, friendship or fun will only come through getting something – and getting it now! It is usually an empty promise.

Prayer

We pray for all those trapped in a web of debt who find it hard to break free,
who are fearful of further demands for payment and don't know how to cope.
Bring them wise counsel, good judgement and ultimately financial freedom.

We pray for all those involved with helping people to manage their finances better.
Give them generous love, patience and wisdom as they help people negotiate their financial problems.

---

37. Accessed 24 November 2013.
38. Accessed 24 November 2013.

Help us all to be content and to appreciate what we have been given and to resist the temptation to spend money we do not have. Help us to save and to plan for the future rather than just to live for today. And allow us to see money as a tool to be used and not a master to serve.
Amen.

Difficult relationships

Alison Moore

Story

Dana's life felt like hell – the neighbours were playing music all the time through the night. She had spoken to them very politely. They had apologised. Nothing had changed. She asked them again. They said they had turned it down and didn't see there was a problem. She felt so angry now and raged at their inconsiderateness. She was anxious, she rehearsed endless discussions in her head, she couldn't sleep because she was waiting for the music to start. She felt a wreck. She obtained anxiety pills from the doctor and eventually moved house.

Norman's difficult relationship was with his colleague. The younger man arrived at the school as an inexperienced teacher, awkward and shy. Norman, a few years ahead of him and in the same maths department, had befriended him, inviting him for a drink after work, sitting with him at lunchtime and generally looking out for him. He'd anticipated that John would soon find his feet as he got used to the school. A year on, however, John had become even more dependent, and limpet-like seemed to appear at his side whenever Norman wasn't actually teaching. With a sinking heart, Norman realised that John thought of him as his closest friend. How could he possibly manage to distance himself from the relationship? He felt completely trapped.

The nature of the problem

Everyone has difficult relationships – yours will be different from mine. The difficulty may originate from the personality of the other person or from their actions. How difficult the relationship is will depend on how much it impacts your life. This in turn depends on the frequency of contact and the significance of the relationship. Ongoing difficult relationships are likely to evoke a frustrating sense of powerlessness. There may be a genuine power differential – a manager, organiser, teacher or priest; or no obvious power difference – a family member, neighbour or fellow member of the congregation. The impact can range from mild irritation to the all-consuming anger felt by Dana or the imprisonment felt by Norman.

Relationships can be experienced as difficult if there is what psychologists call 'projection' or 'transference' going on. Projection involves one person 'projecting' their own unrecognised feelings or attributes on to someone else. It is then conveniently possible to dislike and blame the other for certain qualities while denying their existence in oneself. Transference takes place when someone reacts to the other *as if* they were someone else they have known. Dana's neighbours may be reminding her of her younger twin brothers, who spent most of their childhood dreaming up ways of making her life a misery. All attempts to get her parents to intervene on her behalf failed as she wasn't taken seriously. Without realising it, she is responding to her neighbours just as she did to her brothers when she was a young teenager.

Sometimes the other person is unclear about their own boundaries, and this can be a major contributor to difficult relationships. For example, they may be unskilled at reading the social clues that most people take for granted. This may well have been the case for John, who mistook Norman's genuinely friendly actions as an invitation to constant companionship.

Its implications

Experiencing an ongoing difficult relationship can be a source of shame ('Why can't I deal with this?'), anger ('Why won't they go away?') or secrecy ('I can't talk about this as it's too embarrassing' or 'It's wrong to make a fuss about something so trivial'). As both Norman and Dana found, a difficult relationship can come to dominate a person's life.

Churches are rife with difficult relationships. It is a myth that churches are places of peace and love, where Christians living in harmony never experience difficult relationships. In fact, both the Old and New Testaments describe endless difficult relationships of one kind or another. The famous verse that appears to reassure about unity, 'Where two or three are gathered in my name, I am there among them' (Matthew 18:20), is found in a chapter entirely given to describing different kinds of conflict. Contrary to our hopes, difficult relationships are normal and to be expected, inside and outside the Church. Unity, love and peace grow through addressing difficult relationships, not by avoiding or denying them.

What might help

The pastoral listener can help to identify the kind of 'difficult relationship' that is going on. It is not helpful to minimise the situation: 'Don't worry about it,' 'They probably don't mean it,' or 'Just ignore them.' Nor is it helpful to offer solutions: to Dana, 'Why don't you get better earplugs?' or 'You just need to pray for the neighbours;' or to Norman, 'It's only at work. John doesn't bother you at home,' or 'Why don't you just tell him you can't spend so much time with him?' Nor does simple collusive agreement help: 'Your neighbours are such malicious people;' 'John is impossible.'

However, you can help your friend or congregation member in other ways: by taking seriously the emotional impact of the difficult relationship; by distinguishing between the person and their role or between the character and the behaviour; by untangling whether there is projection or transference going on, and therefore whether the difficulty lies more with them or with the other. If the other person is really unable to understand or respect normal social boundaries, you can help your friend decide on what boundaries are needed and talk through how to set them in place and keep them; you can recommend assertiveness techniques and help him practise them. You can help Dana think through what her options are, and if necessary what local resources might be available from the council or a lawyer.

Agencies and sources of help

Bridge Builders (www.bbministries.org.uk)[39] is a Christian organisation that works specifically with conflict in churches. It runs practical and high-quality training on leadership and on conflict transformation. Although focused on Christian settings, the principles are applicable to other contexts. There are useful resources on their website. See, for example, the article 'Dealing with conflict in the church – insight from the New Testament' by Colin Patterson.

Self-awareness helps: look for supervision or a supportive conversation partner to help you work out your own contribution to a difficult relationship. Supervision will also help you work out what is going on in any situation where you are supporting someone else.

Assertiveness training is helpful. Good assertiveness training emphasises learning how to give clear and calm messages about what you think and want to do. It helps people move from feeling powerless to being able to express what they really want.

A brief and helpful introduction to the subject is *Dealing with Difficult People* by Jocelyn Bryan, one of the 'Christian Handbook' series.[40]

39. Accessed 22 November 2013.
40. Published by Kevin Mayhew, 2009.

Prayer

Lord God,
thank you for the spectrum of people in your world.
Help me to welcome difference,
to stand up for justice as well as peace,
to see beyond the difficult behaviour,
to be part of the solution rather than part of the problem,
and to love in spite of everything.
Give grace and hope, courage and determination to all whose lives are distorted and blighted by difficult relationships.
For Jesus' sake,
Amen.

Discrimination in the workplace

John Parr

Story

Adrian Smith worked as a manager with Trafford Housing Trust in Manchester. In February 2011, he used his Facebook page to post a comment next to a BBC News Online story with the headline, 'Gay church "marriage" set to get the go-ahead'. According to Mr Smith, gay weddings in churches would be 'an equality too far'. He added, 'If the state wants to offer civil marriages to the same sex then that is up to the state; but the state shouldn't impose its rules on places of faith and conscience.'

Mr Smith's employers believed that his action broke Trafford Housing Trust's code of conduct, even though his comments were not visible to the general public and were posted outside working hours. In their eyes his views might upset his colleagues. He was demoted from his managerial position, his salary was cut by 40 per cent and he was given a final written warning.

Mr Smith sued his employers for breach of contract, claiming that the Trust broke the law by demoting him. In November 2012, Mr Justice Briggs, a High Court judge, ruled in his favour at Manchester Crown Court, saying that his Facebook postings fell short of misconduct and that the Trust's disciplinary actions constituted a breach of contract. On a technicality Mr Smith was awarded damages of just £100. In his summing up, the judge remarked, 'Mr Smith was taken to task for doing nothing wrong, suspended and subjected to a disciplinary procedure which wrongly found him guilty of gross misconduct . . . a conclusion that his damages are limited to less than £100 leaves the uncomfortable feeling that justice has not been done.'

In his statement Mr Smith said, 'I didn't do this for the money – I did this because there is an important principle at stake. Britain is a free country where people have freedom of speech, and I am pleased that the judge's ruling underlines that important principle.'

The chief executive of Trafford Housing Trust, Matthew Gardiner, issued a statement that accepted the court's decision and made a 'full and sincere apology' to Mr Smith. However there was no mention of reinstating or compensating him[41].

---

41. *Guardian*, 16 November 2012: http://www.bbc.co.uk/news/uk-england-manchester-20357131 (accessed 8 December 2013).

Workplace discrimination and inequality

Workplace discrimination occurs when individuals or groups of people are adversely treated in places where they work, during recruitment processes or in employment decisions. Discriminatory treatment is based not on individual merit but on a person's condition or status, as indicated by (among other things) gender, race, age, appearance, religion or belief, sexual orientation, disability, marital status, pregnancy or trade union membership.

This kind of discrimination is often subtle, indirect and ambiguous. At an interview an employer may make a decision based not on the criteria set out in a job description or person specification but on the more subjective judgement as to whether the applicant would fit into the organisation's 'work culture'. A *Newsweek* survey in 2010 advised women to 'work on their appearance to look relevant and promotable', but women also know that they can be disadvantaged for being too attractive.

Workplace discrimination is against the law in many parts of the world. The relevant UK legislation is the Equality Act (2010),[42] which gathered up existing equality law. The Act forbids less favourable treatment in the workplace and wider society on the basis of nine 'protected characteristics': age, disability, gender, gender reassignment, marriage/civil partnership, pregnancy and maternity, race, religion or belief, and sexual orientation. Also forbidden is indirect discrimination, for example in a job advertisement for applicants over a certain height, which would discriminate against women or members of some racial groups. The Act allows certain exceptions, when, for example, it is an occupational requirement that a minister in a Christian church is a Christian, or that a female actor should play a female role.

Research quoted in The Final Report of the Equalities Review highlights a number of areas of workplace inequality, some of which are the result of discrimination:[43]

- Women working full-time earn 83 per cent of what men earn for doing the same work, despite being equally qualified. Women working part-time earn 32 per cent less per hour than women working full-time, and 41 per cent less per hour than men working full-time.
- Women from minority ethnic groups experience additional workplace discrimination. For example, in the UK in the early 2000s Pakistani and Bangladeshi women were 30 per cent less likely to be employed than white men or women (this figure

42. See www.homeoffice.gov.uk/equalities/equality-act (accessed 23 November 2013).
43. 'Fairness and Freedom: The Final Report of the Equalities Review', HMSO 2007, pp.62-74.

has remained constant over a 30-year period). For men from the same ethnic groups the figure was 12 per cent. Research shows that women from these ethnic groups have a positive attitude towards work, and that they are three to four times more likely than their white peers to accept jobs for which they are over-qualified.
- A partnered mother with a child aged under 11 is 45 per cent less likely to be in work than a partnered man. Men's employment rates are not affected by fatherhood.
- A survey of 122 recruitment agencies revealed that more than 70 per cent had been asked by clients to avoid hiring pregnant women or those of childbearing age.
- Disabled people are 29 per cent less likely to be in employment than non-disabled people. Among those who are disabled, people with mental health conditions and learning disabilities have the lowest employment rates. Disabled men earn between 9 per cent and 17 per cent less than non-disabled men (women: 6 per cent to 11 per cent less). Disabled people are more likely to work part-time and less likely to receive training.

Other well-documented areas of inequality in the UK that could be caused in part by discrimination include:
- the disproportionate number of women in low-paid but relatively secure positions in education and health care
- the 'glass ceiling' that sees fewer women in senior positions in companies and universities and as Members of Parliament in the UK
- the Church of England's exclusion of women from the House of Bishops, and so-called 'practising' homosexual people from its priesthood and other positions of leadership
- migrant farm labourers who are forced to work long hours and live in poor-quality accommodation provided by the agencies who recruit them
- domestic workers who are excluded from employment protection
- employees who are not allowed to wear items of clothing or jewellery that have religious significance
- contract cleaners who do not receive the same benefits as a company's workforce, even though they work on the same premises
- a black football coach who has won accolades in the North American Soccer League but has had only one reply to his many applications for coaching or managerial positions with English clubs.[44]

44. Stuart James, 'Racism still exists – it's why there are so few black managers', *Guardian*, 19 December 2012.

The most obvious reason for avoiding workplace discrimination is that it is illegal. In addition, discrimination can adversely affect an organisation's reputation and make it more difficult to retain highly qualified staff. By contrast, offering equal opportunities promotes job satisfaction, and by respecting diversity it contributes towards the creation of a more harmonious society.

Pastoral wisdom

A wise pastor will want to support a person who believes they are experiencing discrimination in the workplace by ensuring that they make informed responses to the situation. If the issue cannot be resolved informally, the employee should consult the employer's written grievance procedure, which sets out the responsibilities of both parties in the case of a dispute and guides employees through the appropriate procedures. Where the employee is a member of a trade union, this body would provide advice and support. Where this is not the case, the Citizens Advice Bureau or an advocacy or mediation service may be an alternative.

Sources of help

- The Advisory, Conciliation and Arbitration Service (ACAS) (www.acas.org.uk)[45]
- The Equality Advisory Support Service, provided by the Equality and Human Rights Commission (www.equalityhumanrights.com/about-us/equality-advisory-support-service)[46]

Prayer

God our Father,
in your Son Jesus Christ you reveal your love
as generous, hospitable and indiscriminate.
Teach us to know our own hearts,
and forgive us when we treat others unfairly;
strengthen us to stand with those who experience discrimination
and, whenever we are treated wrongly,
give us the courage, resilience and wisdom
that come as gifts of your Spirit.
Amen.

45. Accessed 23 November 2013.
46. Accessed 23 November 2013.

Drugs

Rupert Bristow

Stories

Under the veneer of the respectability of church, of business, of good works, lurks the perpetual threat of good people (and bad) succumbing to drugs and drink. At the same time, beneath the dirt and sweat of apparent vagrants and addicts may be the flame of the human spirit and the delicate flower of a new start. We owe it to individuals in both categories who seek out the help of the church to support, encourage and pray for a transformation in their lives which can sustain that commitment to a new way.

The question of which substances are harmful, illegal or beyond the pale is so dependent on a particular culture, society, time or set of legal practices that there are no absolutes in this area, though awareness of the current legal categories of drugs is important. What clearly has been around for ever is the temptation to seek sensations induced through available substances, narcotics or concoctions. There are also frequent warnings in the Bible, such as, 'Wine is a mocker, strong drink a brawler, and whoever is led astray by it is not wise' (Proverbs 20:1) and, more obliquely, 'No one can serve two masters; for a slave will either hate the one and love the other, or be devoted to the one and despise the other' (Matthew 6:24).

Take a hard look at the community in which you live. Ask around the agencies, statutory and voluntary, even talk to fellow congregation members. Beneath the surface of most of these networks and communities will be stories of hardship and heartache, and possibly tragedy, because of the use and abuse of drugs. But there will also be heart-warming stories of help and determination to get out of addiction, to reverse the spiral of decline, to set aside a life in thrall to drugs and drug pushers and to take up a life-affirming allegiance to Christ.

Statistics

An estimated one in three adults has taken an illegal drug in their lifetime, according to the latest figures from the Home Office,[47] but

47. https://www.gov.uk/government/publications/drug-misuse-declared-findings-from-the-2011-to-2012-crime-survey-for-england-and-wales-csew-second-edition (accessed 5 December 2013).

the number of people aged 16 to 59 taking drugs is at one of the lowest levels since 1996.[48] The 2011/12 Crime Survey for England and Wales (CSEW) has found that around 12 million people have tried an illicit drug in their lifetime, with the percentage rising slightly from 36.3 per cent in 2010/11 to 36.5 per cent in 2011/12. The number of adults who had taken drugs in the previous year, however, fell to 8.9 per cent – the lowest figure since the measurements began in 1996.

Cannabis remains the most frequently used drug with 2.3 million users taking it in the past year. Powder cocaine and ecstasy were the second and third most prevalent drugs, with 0.7 million and 0.5 million users respectively. However at 6.9 per cent, cannabis use now remains at the lowest level since the CSEW measurement began. Amphetamine use has seen a large fall over the long term, according to the findings, from 3.2 per cent in 1996 down to 0.8 per cent in the 2011/12 survey.

The most common age for first taking powder cocaine, ecstasy or cannabis was between 16 and 18 years old. The most common age for cannabis was 16 whilst for powder cocaine and ecstasy it was 18. The report also found a wide variation for the age of first drug use, from as young as seven up to 57 years old.

Causes and sources

Those surveyed who had used drugs in the past year most commonly obtained drugs from domestic settings such as their own home or from someone else's home. One in five (21 per cent) obtained drugs at a bar, club, party or rave. Locations also differed by drug – cannabis was most likely to have been obtained under domestic circumstances whereas those taking cocaine or ecstasy were more likely to have obtained the drugs at a bar, club, party or rave.

Alcohol would seem to be another contributing factor – adults who reported drinking alcohol three or more days per week were around three times more likely to have used drugs (12.4 per cent) and around six times more likely to have used a Class A drug (4.9 per cent) in the past year than those who had not drunk any alcohol in the last month.

Help

A good place to start is a visit to a GP, who can discuss concerns, assess the nature of the problem and help choose the most

48. http://www.theguardian.com/society/2012/sep/27/illicit-drugs-out-of-fashion (accessed 5 December 2013).

appropriate treatment. A GP might offer to treat or might refer to a local specialist drug service. Many drug treatment services accept self-referrals so, if patients are not comfortable talking to their GP, they might be able to approach the local drug treatment service directly.

Information about local drug treatment services can be found on the Frank website (http://www.talktofrank.com/)[49] or the free Frank drugs helpline can be reached on 0300 123 6600. An adviser can talk through the different options.

Clients who are seen at a local drug treatment service will first be assessed and, if deemed appropriate for treatment, will be allocated a key worker. That key worker may be a doctor, a nurse or a drugs worker. They will help organise the treatment that is needed, develop a personalised care plan and be the first point of call throughout treatment, as well as providing regular one-to-one sessions during the course of treatment.

Outside the NHS, there are many voluntary sector and private drug and alcohol treatment organisations that can help. As well as residential rehab centres, community services of various types are provided by voluntary organisations. These include structured day programmes, outreach and harm reduction services, counselling services, aftercare and housing support services. These organisations will usually be linked to NHS services in each area.

The role of treatment is to enable drug workers to help addicts to recover and to help them become free of dependency. They also support addicts to be active citizens, to take responsibility for their children, to earn their own living and to keep a stable home. Drug users who are parents are fast-tracked to help safeguard their children.

One respected and long-standing voluntary agency in this field is Release, 124–128 City Road, London EC1V 2NJ, helpline 020 7324 2989, website www.release.org.uk.[50] Release is the national centre of expertise on drugs and drugs law, and they provide free and confidential specialist advice to the public and professionals. Release also campaigns for changes to UK drug policy to bring about a fairer and more compassionate legal framework to manage drug use in our society.

In a society where drugs ruin lives and can bring untimely deaths, the Christian message is one of hope and rescue rather than condemnation and abandonment.

49. Accessed 5 December 2013.
50. Accessed 10 December 2013.

Prayers

God of hope,
fill with your Holy Spirit
all those who share the pain of addiction
so that they may glimpse your truth
and know your love,
in all their struggles and all their heartache,
so that they can renew their trust in you,
knowing that your love is sure.
Lord, hear us,
as we cry out to you.
Amen.

(From *Prayers for Inclusion and Diversity* by Rupert Bristow, Kevin Mayhew, 2012)

We commit ourselves to continue the struggle against addiction;
to dedicate ourselves to helping our neighbours as ourselves;
to give comfort and support where needed,
and to recover for you, God of grace,
a pastoral hope, a new start,
and a way back,
with the help of your Son, our Saviour,
Jesus Christ.
Amen.

(From *Services for Special Occasions*, Kevin Mayhew, 2012)

Fraud

Roger Preece

What is it?

The smart pick-up truck drove down the vicarage drive. A young man in a high-visibility jacket stepped out. 'We're just doing some surfacing of the roads nearby and have finished a job but have lots of materials left. We'd like to support the church and notice your drive has plenty of potholes.'

The vicar, pleased with the generous offer, asked 'Are you sure there's no charge?'

'Just pay us towards the materials – something like £1 per foot should be OK,' the young man replied.

The vicar, thinking this is still a generous offer, says that would be helpful and goes on his way. On returning mid-morning he finds four workmen putting a thin layer of tar on the drive and sprinkling gravel over the surface. The young man then grabs the vicar and asks him to pace out the distance and help him with the cost as he hasn't got his tape measure. The drive turns out to be 300 feet long and 30 feet wide. The vicar suddenly realises the workmen want £1 per **square** foot and will be requiring £9000 from him. It is not a pleasant experience when something that looks like generosity turns into a scam, bordering on the criminal.

Or consider a lonely widower who receives a message on Facebook from a beautiful young Eastern European woman who just wants to talk, and he becomes emotionally attached to her. The young woman wants to come to England to visit and 'only needs £5000' to sort out a debt problem and to arrange travel and visa arrangements. The money is sent, but no young woman arrives – a cruel fraud trading on someone's emotional vulnerability.

An official letter arrives through the post informing the recipient that they may have won up to £100,000 in a competition. They just have to ring a phone number, which turns out to be a premium rate number that charges £10 for the call. They are offered a prize which is actually worthless.

Fraud comes in many forms and can be directed towards individuals or organisations. We are all vulnerable to fraud when we enter into financial arrangements with a third party whom we trust. Fraud is any action of deception that causes a loss to a person. It could include abuse of a position of trust or concealing information that should have been made available. According to the

National Fraud Authority, in 2012 more than £15.5 billion was lost due to fraud, of which £9.1 billion was individual loss.[51] Part of this was identity fraud with an estimated cost of £3.3 billion.

What are the impacts?

- Fraud destroys trust and leaves people feeling violated, vulnerable and angry.
- Individuals who have been defrauded might find themselves in serious financial difficulties as a result of the fraud.
- Fraud is a violation of a person and can feel as serious as if burglars have entered your own house to steal from you.

What can be done?

- Help the person to identify whether a fraud has been or is being committed.
- Assist the person with dealing with the direct consequences.
- Help the person with the reporting of and pursuit of the fraudster.
- Help to rebuild their confidence and develop the ability to discern the false from genuine.
- Build up personal and financial confidence in individuals to make them less vulnerable.
- Train children and vulnerable adults in the basic principles of keeping themselves safe – passwords, bank details, security, etc.
- Help people to be sensitive in order to work out what is the risk that they might themselves be working for a scam – for example, some pyramid-selling schemes, call-centre work, selling of securities or time shares, or land banking.

We need to enable people to protect themselves from fraud

- Remember the principle that if an offer looks too good to be true, it is almost certainly false.
- Encourage protection of computers and mobiles phones with security software.
- Remind people not to respond to unsolicited emails or letters. They should be encouraged to call the institutions first using the official number they have on file. If responding to an incoming phone call, they should ideally call back on a different phone or after a significant delay. This is to avoid the fraud where an incoming caller stays on the line and falsifies a dialling tone, touch tone and ring tone so that the victim thinks

51. National Fraud Authority – Annual Fraud Authority report, June 2013.

they have phoned their bank, but they are actually still talking to the fraudster.

- Remind people not to give out personal information unless they have checked that the person asking is genuine. One way is to ask the caller information that only they would know. Another is to call them back on another line using the official number. Remember also that websites can be set up that look genuine but are fake. Services like Rapport from Trusteer have a system that validates the authenticity of a website.[52]
- For financial investments and other business transactions, encourage people to obtain independent advice from someone they trust before making any commitment.
- Make sure people remember that they must not be rushed: if it is a good deal today, it will probably still be worthwhile next week. Scammers will try to force them to act now.
- If someone is romantically linked to someone who is asking for money, then they definitely need independent advice. Love can really be blind and there are many lonely hearts fraudsters trying to take advantage of people's emotional vulnerability.

Resources

The Serious Fraud Office have a range of resources on their website, including a facility for the confidential reporting of major frauds. They also include a description of the main type of fraud that they have identified: www.sfo.gov.uk[53]

For more general fraud, Action Fraud provides a contact line, victim support and reporting of different frauds. It is provided by the National Fraud Authority: www.actionfraud.police.uk[54] or call their telephone line 0300 123 2040.

A good resource is the brochure *Scambuster: Your guide to beating the scammers*, published by the Office of Fair Trading: http://www.stopjunkmail.org.uk/features/scams/resources/oft831.pdf[55]

Citizens Advice consumer service: www.adviceguide.org.uk[56]

Local Authority Trading Standards have teams dedicated to dealing with a range of local fraud. The local police can also be consulted.

52. See www.trusteer.com (accessed 17 December 2013).
53. Accessed 17 December 2013.
54. Accessed 17 December 2013.
55. Accessed 24 November 2013.
56. Accessed 24 November 2013.

Meditation

Christians should be able to be as wise as serpents and as innocent as doves (Matthew 10:16). The person who is determined never to be defrauded might have very little trust in other people and may never take risks in their dealings with others. Sometimes even when there is a risk it is all right to proceed, but we should be able to quantify our losses and decide how much we are willing to lose if everything does go wrong. We need to be learn to be wise about the risks involved in dealings with others, to evaluate them and to be able to take quantified risks in trusting others.

We need to be humble and be willing to seek advice from others. This can be difficult when we are emotionally involved in the transaction or don't want to be embarrassed.

Prayer

Heavenly Father,
give me clarity of understanding and wisdom to understand all that might be offered to me.
Give me contentment with what I have, and may I trust you for my needs.
Give me discernment to understand the heart and intention behind people's offers to me.
Let me not become cynical but give people the benefit of the doubt, yet with eyes wide open to the risks.
Protect me from those who have evil intentions towards me;
let them be found out and receive the justice due to them for their deceit.
Let me always be just and honest in my own dealings and to think from the perspective of the relationship with the other.
May all my dealings be seen as just and fair, considerate and not taking unfair advantage of power that I have at my disposal.
Amen.

Generalised anxiety disorder

Bill Merrington

Story

Louise had been in the church all of her life. Right through her childhood she had been a clingy, anxious child, never wanting to leave her mother when the other children went to the Sunday school classes. She remained anxious as an adult. Everyone knew her in church although she was cautious with newcomers. Louise would often come forward for prayer ministry and present various concerns ranging from work to family issues to her own health worries. She was well known to the local medical surgery and although she held down a job, she spent several weeks off work each year. Eventually Louise had a small number of people who would support her whom she came to trust and rely upon. However, many fell by the wayside as they found her demands and anxieties just too taxing to cope with.

Background

Generalised anxiety disorder (GAD) is a common anxiety disorder that involves excessive worrying, nervousness and tension. The anxiety is not related to one cause but seems more diffuse, colouring the person's whole life with dread. In the past this might have been called a neurosis. It is characteristically different from a panic attack, which is more intense and comes in short bursts. A person with GAD might find that their whole day is full of anxiety as they worry about their health, family, work and finance, and at night are unable to sleep. Just the thought about getting through the day can bring on anxiety. It can seem impossible to control these anxieties and they seem to take control of the person.

Everyone worries, but there is usually some control mechanism that restrains the anxiety. For people with GAD, there is often with their anxiety a degree of excessive, intrusive, persistent thoughts that debilitates the person. The person experiences tension in their muscles, has great difficulty falling asleep and then staying asleep. They may have stomach problems, nausea and diarrhoea.

The good news is that everyone reflects a characteristic profile of emotional stability across a spectrum:

Openness – ranging from curious to cautious
Conscientiousness – organised to careless

Extraversion – outgoing to reserved
Agreeableness – compassionate to unkind
Neuroticism – sensitive and nervous to secure and confident

A degree of anxiety is, in fact, healthy, as it proves to be a protective mechanism, making a person aware of potential dangers. So an anxious person might go to the doctor with a small concern and find that they catch an illness before it becomes serious, while a more relaxed individual might fail to seek treatment in time. However, with GAD, the anxiety becomes a pervading intrusiveness into the person's life. It may also be linked with a neuroticism, a psychological behavioural disorder in which anxiety is the primary characteristic. Neuroticism is a long-term tendency to be in a negative emotional state, which can lead to depressive moods.

Causes

While advances have been made in the treatment of GAD, the actual causes are harder to identify. There may be a tendency for a genetic link. It may involve naturally occurring brain chemicals (neurotransmitters), such as serotonin, dopamine and norepinephrine. While everyone has a flight or fight response, people with GAD react in an anxious state that does not warrant such a flight/fight response. Stress may not be the cause of the condition, but it is a common powerful trigger caused by problems at work, family or perhaps through a close bereavement. It is more likely that GAD is caused by a combination of genetic tendencies, which are triggered by an anxious upbringing, perhaps copying parental behaviours, along with the stresses of daily life.

Help

To help anyone with GAD, there is a need to understand what are the root causes of worrying. People tend to think that worrying comes from other people and the events of life but, in fact, worrying is self-generated. The trigger comes from the outside but the internal running dialogue maintains the anxiety itself. The person tends to talk to themselves about things they are afraid of or negative things that might happen. This endless anxiety is unproductive and tends to sap the person mentally and physically.

It is important when working with people with GAD that there is in an open, engaging and non-judgemental manner. There needs to be confidentiality, along with dignity and respect.

Various techniques can be learned to control anxiety. Relaxation exercises tend to be helpful. These might include progressive muscle relaxation, deep breathing, meditation and mindfulness techniques.

Finding ways of enhancing the senses can be useful:

- Sight – going for a walk, appreciating the countryside, painting or taking photographs
- Sound – listening to soothing music, particularly of the ocean, bird song or leaves rustling
- Smell – lighting scented candles, enjoying the smell of flowers or plants outside, breathing clean air or enjoying the smell of fresh bread
- Touching – stroking a pet, enjoying a warm, bubble-filled bath or being wrapped in a warm blanket
- Taste – cooking sensory foods, treating oneself to a favourite meal or enjoying a favourite hot drink

There are other techniques such as AWARE (Accept the anxiety, Watch your anxiety, Act with the anxiety, Repeat the steps, Expect the best). Alternatively, various cognitive behavioural therapies (CBT) can be productive, provided the person is not in too anxious a state before CBT begins.

The church can be helpful, as anxiety is usually worse when the person is alone. The help of others in a controlled way can be beneficial. This involves building a strong support team and knowing whom to call when worries spiral. The person also needs to know whom to avoid, if certain people cause an increase of anxiety and stress. A healthy lifestyle, good diet and plenty of exercise all contribute to a balanced recovery. If self-help support fails, then professional therapy may be necessary alongside additional support. Some medication can be effective for GAD, although this is recommended only as a short-term solution.

Selected agencies

- NHS Choices – website offering advice and support links: www.nhs.uk/conditions/anxiety[57]
- Mind – support agency offering advice and support links: www.mind.org.uk[58]
- Anxiety UK – support, help and information for those with anxiety disorders: anxietyuk.org.uk[59] Tel. 08444 775 774
- Association of Christian Counsellors (ACC) – for information about counselling offered by Christian trained counsellors. acc-uk.org[60] Tel. 0845 1249569

57. Accessed 24 November 2013.
58. Accessed 24 November 2013.
59. Accessed 24 November 2013.
60. Accessed 24 November 2013.

Books

- *Not to Worry* by Gary Vurnum, (Createspace Publications, 2010).
- *Treating Generalized Anxiety Disorder* by Jayne Rygh, & William Sanderson (New York: Guilford Press, 2004).

Prayer

Eternal God, whose son bore our griefs and carried our sorrows,
hear our prayer for those who find the world a worrying place.
Give courage when light seems to fade,
give companionship when surrounded by loneliness.
Calm the heart when fear seems near,
provide control when the mind races,
and invoke a spirit of learning from the past,
that the future might be shaped by your presence and hope.
So may we learn to look away from ourselves
and seek to care for others as you have cared for us.
In Jesus' name we pray.
Amen.

Homosexuality

John Parr

Story

Neil is 20 and has just completed his first year at art college. He has a lot of friends of both sexes and has managed to stay in touch with his closest friends from his schooldays, who were members of a church youth group. Neil had a couple of girlfriends from the group when he was about 15. Although he got on well with them, he never really felt any strong sexual attraction towards either of them.

Pete was also a member of the youth group. He didn't seem to be particularly interested in girls but he was very sociable, and Neil was attracted by his confidence – and the way he dressed. After his relationship with the second girl ended, Neil found himself thinking about Pete a lot. He enjoyed his company. They listened to the same kind of music and went to gigs together whenever they could afford it. Neil's feelings for Pete grew stronger during the summer before he went to college. Pete was very supportive at a time when Neil was finding his relationship with his mum difficult and his dad always seemed to be at work.

Neil started to have sexual fantasies about Pete, and he wondered whether Pete felt the same way about him. Coming home from a gig one night with some friends, Pete asked Neil if he'd like to stop off at his house for a last drink after the others had gone their separate ways. Neil felt he could hardly say no. Much to his disappointment, nothing happened, but that didn't stop his thoughts running riot when he got home, as he wondered about what might have been.

Two hundred miles away at art college, Neil lived away from home for the first time. One of his flatmates, Tony, was openly gay. Tony introduced Neil to Phil at a party, and they began a relationship soon after. Though it ended just before the first-year exams, Neil felt that Phil had helped him to discover his true sexual identity.

Now the term is over and Neil is back at home with his family, working in his old job at the local supermarket. He sees quite a lot of his friends from the youth group, including Pete, who shocks him by introducing him to Miranda. They met at university and have been together for the past nine months.

Away from college, Neil doesn't feel quite as confident about his sexuality. He knows his relationship with Phil wouldn't go down well at home. And he's not sure what his friends would say. He's never heard them question the church minister's strong line on what the Bible says about homosexuality.

Attitudes towards homosexuality

Homosexuality is the enduring disposition of sexual attraction towards members of the same sex as oneself. Rather than a lifestyle choice, it is increasingly understood to be a natural variation on the continuum of human sexuality that includes heterosexuality, bisexuality and asexuality. Some homosexual people prefer to think of themselves as 'gay' or 'lesbian' because 'homosexual' has many negative connotations. It is associated with sexual behaviour rather than feelings, and some people identify themselves as gay or lesbian without having had a sexual experience with a person of the same sex. Likewise, some have had same-sex experience without thinking of themselves as gay or lesbian.

Homosexual activity was criminalised in the UK until 1967, and it is still illegal in many parts of the world. Homosexuality was regarded as a mental illness until the American Psychiatric Association removed it from its diagnostic manual in 1973, and the World Health Organization followed suit in 1992. By contrast, 'gay' and 'lesbian' are generally seen as positive and affirmative terms, though they are used pejoratively by some young people.[61]

Recent surveys suggest that between 2 per cent and 13 per cent of people identify as homosexual in Western societies, with about 2 per cent identifying as bisexual and 1 per cent asexual.[62]

Homosexual orientation is now thought to be the product of nature rather than nurture. According to the Royal College of Psychiatrists it has its origins in the womb, and is the result of the complex interplay of genetic factors and early uterine development rather than parenting or childhood experience. The College sees no good evidence that a homosexual orientation can be altered, and now believes that it is compatible with normal mental health and social development.[63] In its Submission to the Church of England's

61. A survey by the Association of Teachers and Lecturers in 2008 revealed that 'gay' is the most frequently used term of abuse in schools, followed by 'bitch' and 'slag'. See Denise Winterman, 'How "gay" became children's insult of choice', BBC News Magazine, 18 March 2008 http://news.bbc.co.uk/1/hi/magazine/7289390.stm (accessed 23 November 2013).
62. In a UK survey carried out by the *Guardian* in 2008, 6 per cent identified themselves as homosexual or bisexual, though 13 per cent claimed they had experienced some form of same-sex sexual contact (*Guardian*, 26 October 2008). In the same year an exit poll on Election Day in the USA showed 4 per cent identifying as homosexual or bisexual. In September 2010 the UK Office of National Statistics published a lower figure, 1.4 per cent of people over 16. In this survey, just over 94 per cent identified themselves as heterosexual, with 3 per cent saying they didn't know or refusing to answer.
63. See http://www.rcpsych.ac.uk/pdf/rcpsychposstatementsexorientation.pdf (accessed 23 November 2013).

Listening Exercise on Human Sexuality, the College points out that the origins of sexual orientation confer the same rights of sexual expression and social acceptance wherever people belong on the continuum of human sexuality.[64]

Homosexual relationships vary in stability. Research from the United States suggests that more than half the population of gay and lesbian people are currently involved in romantic relationships, with around 20 per cent having been together for more than ten years.[65] Lack of support for such relationships from wider society, family and religious bodies is often cited as a significant contribution to instability.

Denmark was the first country to legalise same-sex relationships, in 1989, and the UK introduced civil partnerships in 2004. Since 2000, 11 countries have legalised same-sex (or 'equal') marriage,[66] and at the time of writing MPs in the UK Parliament have just voted overwhelmingly in favour of equal marriage. It is reasonable to expect that the wide-ranging benefits that heterosexual marriage brings will be extended to gay and lesbian people who marry, not least in the stability it offers to their relationships.

The growing acceptance of equal marriage is a clear sign that attitudes towards homosexuality are changing in many parts of the world, particularly as religious authority declines. Judaism, Christianity and Islam have contributed significantly to the discrimination and marginalisation of homosexual people. The Christianisation of the Roman Empire, the spread of Islam and Christianity into East Asia from the seventh century CE onwards, and the European colonisation of Africa, Latin America and the South Pacific undermined the acceptance of homosexual relationships by indigenous peoples.[67] It would be a mistake, however, to see the Abrahamic religions as consistently and uniformly opposed to homosexuality. Homoerotic themes were celebrated in Islamic literature from the medieval era. Christian cities in northern Italy, such as Florence and Venice, were hospitable to homosexuality until the second half of the thirteenth century. And today Tel Aviv is one of the most gay-friendly cities in the world.

---

64. See. http://www.rcpsych.ac.uk/members/specialinterestgroups/gaylesbian/submissiontothecofe/psychiatryandlgbpeople.aspx#origins (accessed 23 November 2013).
65. American Psychological Association, Sexual Orientation and Marriage, available at http://www.apa.org/about/policy/marriage.aspx (accessed 23 November 2013).
66. Argentina, Belgium, Canada, Denmark, Iceland, Netherlands, Norway, Portugal, Spain, South Africa and Sweden. It is also legal in parts of Brazil, Mexico and the USA.
67. See Stephen Murray and Will Roscoe (eds) (1997), *Islamic Homosexualities: Culture, History, and Literature*, New York: New York University Press, and Stephen Murray and Will Roscoe (1998) Boy-Wives and Female Husbands: Studies of African Homosexualities, New York: St. Martin's Press.

Informing the pastoral response

Pastoral response is informed by three broad areas of concern, which remain even when prejudice-fuelled hostility towards homosexuality is set aside. The first involves the redefinition of marriage implied by same-sex marriage. Current debates in the UK have raised the question of what is essential in a marriage. Those who wish to restrict it to heterosexual relationships see marriage as a loving, exclusive and faithful relationship that provides the context for sexual expression, reproduction and child-rearing. Those who advocate a more inclusive view see the relationship alone as the essential element, and point out that many heterosexual marriages are child free and non-sexual. To those who argue for the adequacy of civil partnerships, advocates of equal marriage reply that all couples should be able to enjoy the same recognition, support and protection under the law. This is evidence of the impact of wider cultural forces on a traditional institution, in this case the reshaping of marriage in a world of equal rights. The fact that gay and lesbian people wish to be married can be taken as a sign of the durability of marriage, and not – as some of its more traditional supporters fear – that it is about to wither.

A second area of concern lies in attempts to change a gay or lesbian person's sexual orientation. These are based on the opinion that homosexuality is either a disorder – a view which is now rejected by informed legal and mental health establishments – or inherently sinful.[68] The Royal College of Psychiatrists questions the quality of the evidence that such change is possible, and highlights the fact that treatments to change sexual orientation succeed only in causing significant psychological damage.[69] But in its helpful statement about sexual orientation, the American Psychological Association acknowledges that 'the emergence, recognition and expression of one's sexual orientation varies among individuals', and that during the period of adolescent development, 'experimentation and discovery are normal and common'.[70] This suggests that for those who are unsure of their sexual orientation, it is possible that sensitive counselling and prayer may be beneficial,

---

68. See the statement issued by the American Psychological Association, 'Just the Facts about Sexual Orientation & Youth: A Primer for Principals, Educators and School Personnel' (2008), available at http://www.apa.org/pi/lgbt/resources/just-the-facts.aspx?item=3 (accessed 23 November 2013).
69. See above, note 4; Peterson Toscano relates the devastating impact of 20 years of gay 'conversion' therapies in 'Gay "conversion" therapies give moral authority to bullies, says ex-missionary', in the *Guardian*, 13 April 2012.
70. 'Just the Facts about Sexual Orientation & Youth: A Primer for Principals, Educators and School Personnel'.

as long as those who offer them adopt a positive and person-centred approach to the development of sexual identity.

A third area of concern is the place of conscience in the face of changing social attitudes. It is important to recognise that many people genuinely find it difficult to change attitudes and beliefs that have been years in the making. This is not to excuse damaging or abusive opinions and behaviour, but rather to acknowledge that it can take time and effort to reshape the outlook of individuals and communities whose strongly held opinions are an essential part of the way they define themselves and construct their world. Conscience is informed by any number of loyalties, and in the fundamental areas of identity surrounding human relationships – of which sexual orientation is just one example – these loyalties can find themselves competing with each other. In such situations many people testify to the decisive impact of encountering 'the other' – the person who is different – rather than argument, however reasonable and well informed. Religious believers of all persuasions should need no convincing of the priority of such encounters in shaping their consciences. And when people from among the world's most vulnerable and marginalised groups are involved, there is always the chance that we will find ourselves on holy ground.

Sources of help

- The Evangelical Fellowship of Lesbian and Gay Christians believes that there is no contradiction in being both homosexual and Christian: www.eflgc.org.uk[71]
- The Lesbian and Gay Christian Movement works for love, peace, justice and the promotion of the Christian faith especially within the LGBT community: www.lgcm.org.uk[72]
- Inclusive Church works for a church that is open to all: www.inclusive-church.org.uk[73]
- Changing Attitude works for inclusion across the Anglican Communion: http://changingattitude.org.uk/[74]
- Stonewall is a campaigning and lobbying organisation promoting equality for lesbians, gay men and bisexuals: www.stonewall.org.uk/[75]

71. Accessed 23 November 2013.
72. Accessed 23 November 2013.
73. Accessed 8 December 2013.
74. Accessed 23 November 2013.
75. Accessed 23 November 2013.

Prayer

God our maker,
you bring us to life in loving relationships
and reveal the breadth of your welcome
and the tenderness of your care
in the generous hospitality of Jesus.
Open our eyes to the wonder and beauty of love
wherever we experience it,
that we may welcome it
as the sure sign of your presence in our world.
Amen.

Illegal immigrants

Rupert Bristow

Story

By the very nature of illegal immigration, case stories are shrouded in mystery. However, there is enough evidence from cases of exploitation, prostitution and human trafficking – effectively modern-day slavery – to indicate that illegal immigrants are often at the mercy of gangs, international criminals and mafia-style organisations, lured into coming here with the promise of a better life and then caught in a trap from which they cannot escape without being exposed as the illegal immigrants they have become. Only in high-profile cases of exposure of these crimes do we hear of the degradation and often inhuman conditions under which they live.

As well as such cases, there are indeed people who have managed to subvert the immigration rules, either totally brazenly or through error and administrative inertia on the part of the UK authorities, whose cases may go to court and for whom deportation may follow, sometimes quite quickly and sometimes after a prolonged delay.

Statistics

Statistics are notoriously difficult to compile, for obvious reasons, but estimates of undocumented immigrants in the UK vary between 310,000 and 863,000.

Causes

Emigration and immigration have as many causes as there are people engaging in the process of leaving one country and going to another. Underlying most cases is the pull of economic migration to a particular country to find a better life, if possible by legal means but, if circumstances allow or dictate, by illegal immigration. Of course, there may also be a need for an individual or a family to flee a country where the person or family, or even ethnic group, perceive a danger to themselves. Here the overwhelming imperative is to get out of a country, which may also mean having to enter another country by non-legal means.

There is therefore an honourable and long history of emigration and immigration affecting most countries and peoples. The holy family of Mary, Joseph and Jesus had to flee into Egypt to avoid

Herod's murderous intentions on all newly born children (Matthew 2:13-15). The Bible is full of one exodus or exile after another. The Israeli people had been harried from pillar to post until their own land was formed after the Second World War – and in its turn that has displaced others.

Great Britain is made up of groups who have come to our shores for a whole host of reasons, from conquering Romans and Normans to immigrants from throughout the British Empire, as was, and then the Commonwealth, to fight for the allied cause, to work in our transport and health systems, to attend our colleges and universities, and to flee civil wars or dictatorships in their own countries. Other immigrants include Jews who came just before the Second World War, Biafrans and Ugandan Asians, Vietnamese boat people and Somalis. Arguably, this pattern of movement and change has greatly enriched our culture, but equally most governments since the war have sought to restrict immigration, except where there are overwhelming moral (e.g. in the case of Ugandan Asians) or legal reasons (as for immigration from other EU members) to permit such an influx.

Help

Anyone presenting their situation to a friend, a church, a voluntary support group or a specialist agency will need and expect a listening ear and an open mind. Most of us cannot easily take in the enormity of the steps taken by individuals which have led to their being here. And it is quite possible that they will have a degree of fear and suspicion about whether they are right to share their situation. At one extreme, a church may be seen as a last resort for someone who has exhausted all the legal processes and sees as their only hope to seek 'sanctuary' in a church, a concept which has a long history but a dubious legality.

There is an added dilemma for an individual, church or organisation to whom someone turns for assistance on immigration or welfare matters when a criminal offence appears to have been committed, as in the case of an illegal immigrant. Should the police be informed? All the more important that reputable and specialist advice agencies are involved at an early stage – and that organisations have clear policies about how to deal with individuals who appear to have broken the law.

There is a host of agencies both national and, in areas where there is an immigrant population, local who can offer that safe point of advice, even if there has to be referral on to a more specialist organisation. However, there are also individuals and organisations purporting to give legal help and assistance who may only be interested in taking money off a client and then not dealing with the matter properly, so caution is necessary!

In many areas there are local migrant support groups or helplines, which could be of great assistance. But respected national bodies also exist, including the Joint Council for the Welfare of Immigrants, which has a long and exemplary record of campaigning and representation:

JCWI
115 Old Street, London, EC1V 9RT
Tel: 020 7251 8708
Fax: 020 7251 8707
Website: www.jcwi.org.uk[76]

Prayers

Lord and Father of humankind,
you sent your Son as a stranger in a hostile world:
born in an outhouse,
shunned by ordinary people,
and killed by the great and the good.
Only the excluded and outcast,
faithful fishermen and loyal womenfolk
welcomed him and took him to their hearts,
as the prophets would have wanted.
So let us learn our lessons and free our hearts
to be accepting of the stranger,
to be open to the different,
to be gracious to the alien,
to be generous to grateful and ungrateful alike.
Help us to be a bit more like your Son,
whose welcome is constant to those who turn to him.
Amen.

Great shepherd of the sheep,
may we be both pastor and friend
to those of a different ethnic origin,
to those of a different sexuality,
to those of a different age,
to those of a different faith,
to those of a different nationality.

76. Accessed 10 December 2013.

As you are alongside the lonely and oppressed,
the minority as well as the majority,
help us to make room in our hearts
to get to know the different in your world,
because we all share in one bread,
the bread of life.
Amen.

(From *Prayers for Parishes* by Rupert Bristow, Kevin Mayhew, 2011)

Infidelity

Alison Moore

Story

How could she ever trust him again? It turned out that he had been lying for months about his heavy work commitments. Tina had believed him – felt sorry for him even. She had explained Pete's absence at church meetings, she'd supported the children through their exams, she'd taken over all the domestic arrangements, booked the holiday, serviced the car. And she'd still be believing him now if her friend Mel from church hadn't told her that she'd seen him walking on the beach one afternoon with his arm around a young woman. Shocked and disbelieving, she'd checked up on him and found more evidence. After sleepless nights, she finally confronted him and he admitted it. It was someone from work, and it had been going on for 11 months.

She explained to Mel between sobs that it wasn't just that she felt stupid for not seeing it, dirty for having had sex with him while he was sleeping with someone else, unattractive and ashamed because he preferred another woman . . . but also that she had lost everything: self-respect, the man she thought she knew inside out, all the good memories of the year, which were false, the secure future together, the trustworthy father, the good and moral Christian. Now Pete was begging her to forgive him and give the marriage another chance.

The nature of the problem

Infidelity happens. It can happen in the most settled of marriages and in the most Christian of contexts. 'I'm not the sort of person who would have an affair,' people declare, baffled with themselves because they just have. The reality is that infidelity, unfaithfulness, 'having an affair', doesn't happen only to 'certain sorts of people'. It can happen to anyone.

Infidelity, which involves breaking the marriage vow of faithfulness to the marriage partner, covers a wide spectrum: from a casual encounter after too much alcohol, regretted as soon as it is over, to serial sexual relationships run in parallel with marriage; from an intense, brief, emotional involvement with a colleague to a serious, long-term, deep relationship that is like a secret second marriage. Infidelity usually means sexual unfaithfulness, but many people have stories to tell about losing their partner to work, the computer, a hobby, the church, a good friend. No sex is involved, but the emotional focus has moved away from the marriage partner, leaving a sense of loss and betrayal that is very real, although more difficult to describe.

For many people affected by infidelity, it is the betrayal that hits the hardest, and rebuilding trust is often the biggest challenge. When infidelity is revealed in a church context, there are added layers of complexity. Shock, judgement, shaken belief, moral concern, compassion, outrage, and so on: sexual behaviour carries a powerful emotional charge, as a congregation experiences different reactions simultaneously.

Its implications

Sexual infidelity doesn't come from nowhere. There is always a context. Uncomfortably for both, but particularly for the 'innocent' party, the affair often says something about the marriage relationship. If Tina and Pete are able to talk honestly with each other once the initial shock has died down, they may look back and see how much they have been on separate tracks since their children were born ten years ago. They stopped sharing much with each other for good reasons, each wanting to protect the other from extra worries. They gradually each lost confidence in themselves: Tina felt she was boring and unattractive, exhausted by teaching assistant work, children and the household; Pete felt he was an inept father and husband who got everything wrong when he arrived home, exhausted by work and the journey. From here it was easy to make assumptions about the other: Tina assumed Pete wasn't interested in her or the family; Pete assumed Tina didn't need him.

After infidelity, each partner will have a different, sometimes contradictory, emotional path to travel towards a restored relationship. The unfaithful one is ready to put the past behind and work towards a new future; the other is still in shock, probably wanting to ask questions, trying to come to terms with the full impact of what has happened. This is a demanding time.

What might help

The pastoral carer needs to listen to both sides, if necessary imagining what the other person's position might be. She will remind herself that there will be a background context out of which the events have unfolded. While listening to all the emotions that are being expressed, she will avoid making any condemning remarks. She won't be afraid to mention sex. She will be aware of children's needs, and others affected in the circle of family and friends. She will keep an eye open for any practical support that is required. If she is supporting the partner who is still in shock, she may find descriptions of normal responses to loss and grief useful to refer to.

Agencies and sources of help

Grief responses are described in different diagrammatic forms. The 'grief wheel', or Elisabeth Kübler-Ross' 'Five stages of grieving', for example, are easily found via the web.

Couple counselling agencies

Counselling can be helpful if a couple or one partner wants to understand or come to terms with what has happened. When a couple wants to rebuild their relationship, the counselling environment can offer a safe place to have difficult conversations.

Relate: www.relate.org.uk[77]

Marriage Care: www.marriagecare.org.uk[78]

Scripture

> Do not fear, for I have redeemed you;
> I have called you by name, you are mine.
> When you pass through the waters, I will be with you;
> and through the rivers, they shall not overwhelm you.
>
> *Isaiah 43:1-2*

> As God's chosen ones, holy and beloved, clothe yourselves with compassion, kindness, humility, meekness, and patience. Bear with one another and, if anyone has a complaint against another, forgive each other; just as the Lord has forgiven you, so you also must forgive.
>
> *Colossians 3:12-13*

77. Accessed 22 November 2013.
78. Accessed 22 November 2013.

Prayer

Heavenly Father,
your Son Jesus Christ knew what it was to be betrayed and abandoned by his closest friends.
Be with those who have experienced the pain and powerlessness of infidelity in their marriage;
give them comfort and hope, supportive friends and renewed relationships.
Your apostle and friend Peter knew what it was to betray the one he loved.
Be with those who have, by their actions and choices, wounded and hurt those close to them;
may they, like Peter, be able to face the reality of what they have done, know your presence, seek forgiveness, and work to restore good relationships.
We ask in the name of Jesus and in the power of the Spirit, who leads into all truth.
Amen.

Marriage breakdown

Alison Moore

Story

After 30 years of marriage, Sue is beginning a new life, not of her own choosing. She was married at 18 to John, and for the last 20 years they have lived in tied accommodation with their working lives intertwined: he as handyman and she as housekeeper at a large, residential, church-run youth centre. Sue's matronliness comforted and amused everyone alike. Sue is chatty, bubbly and opinionated, in contrast to John's quiet and withdrawn manner, and she always seemed to be the dominant one in the relationship. Not having their own children was a sadness to them both.

Over the years, John developed an interest in local history, and would spend hours online and with the local history group. There he became friends with Dawn. She is even quieter than he is, and draws from him a protective and nurturing response he hadn't known he was capable of. He realised that he and Sue had been in a stagnant rut for years. He had never dared challenge her loud assumptions and opinions, and is blossoming by being with someone with whom he can have open and intelligent discussions.

Within a year, John had handed in his notice and left Sue for Dawn, and a new job at a school in the next town where Dawn lives. The handyman who replaced him came with a young family so the church needed the house for him. Sue couldn't face continuing the job with so many memories, and she felt such shame in her church because of her situation, so she moved to the other side of town. She works in a supermarket during the day and cleans at a care home in the early mornings to afford the rent she now has to pay.

The nature of the problem

Some say that the statistics speak for themselves. The last available figures show that more than 30 per cent of marriages will end in divorce. Cohabiting couples also often experience breakdown after long and committed relationships. In any congregation, everyone will know someone whose marriage has broken down – their own or that of a neighbour, a family member or a friend. Although the experience is now so common as to hardly raise an eyebrow, for the people involved – and those in the circles around them – it is always disruptive and usually painful. A couple who have been together for even a few years have created a shared life, woven together.

Breakdowns happen in different ways and for different reasons. External reasons can include increasingly separate lives, work-focused timetables and severely pressurised jobs. Internal reasons can include growing apart, unrealistic expectations of emotional support or intimacy, a shift in the internal dynamics when one partner changes, becoming stuck in 'ruts' or behaviour patterns. To outsiders the story may look clear, and friends can easily be drawn into believing a simplistic narrative. 'John had an affair – how could he treat Sue like that? That poor woman, after all she did for him.' Or, 'Why didn't he leave Sue years ago? How did he put up with her constantly nagging him?'

In churches, complications increase when a church's stance is very judgemental about marriage break-up. It's as if churches preach – and believe in – forgiveness and a new start *unless* a marriage break-up is involved.

Its implications

The psychological and soul work needing to be done after a breakdown is different for each party. It is particularly hard for the partner who did not choose to end the marriage, and who, like Sue, is therefore unable to decide their own future.

Church members, families and friends might take sides and make judgements. Previous friends melt away. Social situations become awkward – women newly single find they are no longer welcome as friends of married men in the church; men newly single can be cosseted and pitied. Partners now on their own experience multiple losses. Sue has lost a marriage partner, friend, lover, job, family relationships, home, habits, friends, income, status, social life and shared future. The adjustments are multi-layered. John has also lost a lot, but for now at least his gains will significantly outweigh the losses: new love, home, companionship, happiness, job, family and friends.

What might help

Those around need to remember that it 'takes two to tango', and that despite appearances, marriage breakdown rarely comes from nowhere. This doesn't mean condoning someone's hurtful or irresponsible actions, but it does help to resist being drawn into condemnation or name calling. Parents live to regret insulting the absent son- or daughter-in-law in the heat of the moment when the couple later make it up.

Pastoral carers in particular help best by positioning themselves, literally or metaphorically, equidistant from each person in the couple so that they can 'see' both the partners. After hearing graphic descriptions of what the absent partner has done, they would do well to remember that if they met the other party they would hear a different story.

On a very practical level, after a marriage breakdown, friends can remember to include the newly single person in their social life, to offer help to the now solo parent, to be thoughtful about the needs of those affected in a secondary way. For example, children may now have to split their time between two homes and adjust to stepsiblings; wider family members may have less or awkward contact with a previously loved and included member; parents-in-law may be heartbroken.

Agencies and sources of help

Organisations specialising in relationship counselling that offer support before, during or after a break-up; they will see one partner:

- Relate: www.relate.org.uk[79]
- Marriage Care: www.marriagecare.org.uk[80]

NHS counselling: It is worth discussing with your GP the possibility of referral to NHS counselling services.

'Relate Guides' is a series of self-help books, including *Moving On – Breaking up without breaking down* by Suzie Hayman.[81]

Scripture and prayer

> He heals the broken-hearted, and binds up their wounds.
>
> *Psalm 147:3*

> . . . be kind to one another, tender-hearted, forgiving one another, as God in Christ has forgiven you.
>
> *Ephesians 4:32*

Heavenly Father,
you created us and made us to find meaning and joy in our lives through our relationships.
We remember all whose marriages have broken down, where hope has been disappointed and love has been lost.
Where there is sadness and grief, bring healing and love;
where there is anger and hurt, renew hope and joy.
Open new treasures for them
through the love of Jesus Christ
and the power of the Holy Spirit.
Amen.

---

79. Accessed 22 November 2013.
80. Accessed 22 November 2013.
81. Published by Vermilion, 2001.

Ouija boards

Ed Hone

Attempting to contact the spirits of the departed using a Ouija board can be similar to a light-hearted party game, or it can be a terrifying encounter with the unknown. Essentially the board is simply a mechanism which facilitates the spelling out of messages supposedly from the spirit world; it can be purpose-made or improvised. A popular home-made Ouija board employs an upturned wine glass and either lettered or numbered cards. Each participant places a hand or finger on the glass, and then waits for it to move towards the cards. Amongst participants there are often some who believe in the supernatural aspect of the experience, and some who believe it is entirely controlled by those present, consciously or not.

Are they harmful?

There are several aspects of playing with Ouija boards that should concern the Christian and inform the Christian pastoral approach: those are spiritual, psychological and practical. There is no place in the Christian belief system for communicating with the departed. Christians do believe in life after death, of course, but not in the presence of disembodied spirits attempting to communicate with the living. In fact, the Christian is very much at home with the idea of the supernatural: of a world beyond what we can experience with our senses – that is, with the world of faith. Even belief in the communion of saints – those who have died in Christ – does not allow for this two-way conversation. At best, then, in the spiritual sense, using a Ouija board in an attempt to consult with departed spirits is based on false spiritual premises and time-wasting; at worst, it can seriously undermine a healthy approach to living life and faith.

As with other occult practices, using Ouija boards can be psychologically harmful, both demonstrating and strengthening a morbid preoccupation. Belief that a spirit is in fact communicating through the board can play on subconscious fears of, for example, the malign influence of spirits and even possession by spirits. Whilst the pastor can support and advise here, it may be necessary to refer a person who is badly affected by a Ouija-board séance to a qualified counsellor or therapist.

It is worth noting that it is not uncommon for teenagers to experiment with Ouija boards, having seen them used in supernatural thrillers, for example. The potential of psychological turmoil that could be triggered in this instance, at a time when so much else is occurring during the life of an adolescent, is something clearly to be avoided. No contact, or no further contact, with Ouija boards is clearly the only sensible advice for the pastor to give.

On a more mundane level, Ouija boards can be used deliberately to frighten, coerce or otherwise manipulate the behaviour of others: if one person in the group so chooses, they can steer the result of the séance whilst claiming the message is from an invisible spirit.

The clearest pastoral pointers here are to be non-judgemental if someone has used a Ouija board, firm about their potential harmfulness, and supportive in helping them if they have been hurt by Ouija board use.

Scripture

The Christian life is focused on God

> One thing I asked of the Lord,
> that will I seek after:
> to live in the house of the Lord
> all the days of my life,
> to behold the beauty of the Lord,
> and to inquire in his temple.
>
> *Psalm 27:4*

Prayer

Loving God, may the Holy Spirit of your Son
guide us and keep us safe.
May our gaze be on you, and on you alone,
that we may rejoice in your presence for ever.
Help us speak of your goodness
to those who are lost, lonely and confused,
that they may recognise that you alone are God.
Through the same Christ our Lord.
Amen.

Prison

Ed Hone

Infamous

The Loneliest Man in the World[82] tells the story of one of the most infamous prisoners of the twentieth century – Rudolf Hess. The book, written by the prison's warden, tells the story of seven Nazis convicted at the Nuremburg trials and imprisoned in Spandau in West Berlin. For the final 20 years of his life, Hess was the only prisoner in Spandau, and the gaol was demolished after his death in 1987.

In a starkly symbolic way, Hess's story reveals the function of prison: to punish crime by depriving the criminal of their liberty. This is the most obvious role of prisons; they also remove from wider society those who might pose a danger to others, and serve as warnings to other and would-be criminals that, if caught, they too will be punished. If this were the whole story, then pastoral care of prisoners would be limited to ministering to their immediate spiritual needs, without regard for their wider needs. However, there are other, vitally important aspects to prison, especially noteworthy for Christians: prison is for reflection, rehabilitation and renewal of life.

Jesus specifically includes visiting those in prison in his teaching on the last judgement. He observes that when ministering to those in prison, the disciple is ministering to Christ himself: such is his identification with those in need. Even in his final agony on the cross, Jesus showed compassion to the thief suffering beside him, promising him a place in Paradise. So for the Christian, ministering to those in prison is mandated by the Lord.

Issues

It is important to note the complexities of life associated with prison: not all prisoners are guilty of crime, for example – some are on remand, awaiting trial. Others know they are serving long sentences and that they have little chance of being released. Prisons vary enormously, from high-security to open prisons, from Victorian institutions to modern facilities; so, too, the issues faced by prisoners vary from place to place, from person to person. Ministry must take account of this complexity if it is to be effective in at least partly meeting the needs of those who ask for help.

---

82. Bird, Eugene K, *The Loneliest Man in the World,* Martin Secker & Warburg Ltd, 1974.

There are a number of basic points that are good to remember in everyday dealings with those in prison, those awaiting trial and those who have been released, as well as the families affected by prison. Imprisonment should not mean that a person loses their dignity or the right to be treated with respect. The punitive element of imprisonment should be balanced with the rehabilitative; this is where the quality of a person's contact with life 'on the outside' will lessen their chance of reoffending. Opportunities for education, similarly, are important in enhancing life in prison and after prison. The role of the pastor as 'befriender', someone who is perceived to be supportive of the person in prison, can play a significant role in humanising the experience of prison. Having someone to confide in, someone who can be trusted, someone who seeks to help rather than condemn is likely to help rehabilitation after prison. The pastor needs a sense of compassion and must to be able to avoid over-identifying with the person to whom (with whom) they are ministering. It is also important to maintain an appropriate distance where necessary, as well as an objective, if sympathetic, ear. This objectivity is not coldness nor an unfeeling indifference, but rather retaining the ability to see the needs of others in context and therefore to be able to respond more fully.

Life after prison

Being released from prison can bring its own problems: facing the social stigma of having been 'inside', trying to find employment whilst having a criminal record, financial hardship and rebuilding relationships that may have suffered because of separation and lack of communication. Attending to this area of ministry is of vital pastoral concern, not just for the individual but for their wider social network. Here, social services can have a part to play, as can various organisations and self-help groups. Churches can offer practical help too, as well as the continual ministry of prayer.

Organisations

Insidetime describes itself as 'the National Newspaper for Prisoners and Detainees', and contains a wealth of articles and news stories for those in the prison system.[83]

One useful section of *Insidetime* offers a full listing of more than 140 organisations that offer help in prison-related fields.[84]

83. insidetime.org (accessed 5 December 2013).

84. http://www.insidetime.org/info-help-results.asp?group=released&do=ListAll (accessed 5 December 2013).

Insideinformation. is a comprehensive guide to prisons and related services.[85] The site (and accompanying book) are designed to help prisoners, their friends and family members and anyone working in a prison-related industry or service. It has been designed with input from former prisoners and includes information supplied by each prison and the organisations whose service details are provided.

Scripture

Ministering to those in need is ministering to Christ

> '. . . for I was hungry and you gave me food, I was thirsty and you gave me something to drink, I was a stranger and you welcomed me, I was naked and you gave me clothing, I was sick and you took care of me, I was in prison and you visited me.' Then the righteous will answer him, 'Lord, when was it that we saw you hungry and gave you food, or thirsty and gave you something to drink? And when was it that we saw you a stranger and welcomed you, or naked and gave you clothing? And when was it that we saw you sick or in prison and visited you?' And the king will answer them, 'Truly I tell you, just as you did it to one of the least of these who are members of my family, you did it to me.'
>
> *Matthew 25:35-40*

Prayer

Lord Jesus,
when we are in need, help us;
when we are weak, give us strength;
when we are confused, guide us;
when we have sinned, forgive us;
when we have plenty, help us to share;
when we see our neighbour in need, help us to serve,
for in serving each other, we serve you.
Amen.

85. http://www.insidetime.org/publications.asp?a=insideinformation&s=info (accessed 5 December 2013).

Redundancy

Ed Hone

Going for broke

The 1997 British film *The Full Monty* portrayed the struggles of six men after they had been made redundant in the face of the collapse of the steel industry in Sheffield. Although a comedy, the movie did not shy away from the personal and social devastation that redundancy, and unemployment in general, can cause. One man's sense of self-worth suffered so much when he lost his job that he became impotent, and his marriage suffered as a result; another was too ashamed to admit to his wife that he was unemployed so he pretended to go to work every day; a third was threatened to lose contact with his son – and so the issues multiplied. The idea that they should do a striptease performance provided the comic relief. This bitter-sweet, black comedy highlighted redundancy as destructive, whilst not sentimentalising it. The true reality of redundancy, however, usually lacks a comic side.

For clarification, redundancy is when an employer reduces its workforce because a job or jobs are seen as no longer necessary: a company restructures, or ceases aspects of its production, or simply scales back its workforce. Work earns us the money to live and helps to support those with whom we live; it can give us a sense of worth, of being useful; it can add to our sense of purpose and even bring personal fulfilment. So when we are told that we are no longer necessary, and that we will not be replaced, it can have a profound effect on us. Like the six men in Sheffield, we can be knocked for six, with a sense of somehow having failed; we are left feeling inadequate, anxious, angry, depressed and disempowered. The more difficult the wider financial outlook is, and the older we are, the bleaker everything can seem. If the redundancy payment is not very substantial, financial worries add to our woes.

What can be said and done?

Firstly, there is no shame in being made redundant: it is our job that has been deemed unnecessary – we are victims of events beyond our control, so self-blame is neither appropriate nor useful. Following on from this, there is no need for feelings of shame, and no point in hiding away from others, as if there was something to keep from them.

The Full Monty also highlights something important: the men encouraged each other, helped each other, found a sense of purpose together, and took control of their own lives as far as they could: they did not remain passive in the face of adverse circumstances. The task of seeking new employment can be daunting and dispiriting, but there are agencies that can help. There are also usually openings for voluntary work which can be taken on for short or longer periods of time, giving a sense of purpose, keeping us in the habit of work and using our own misfortune for the benefit of others. Networking is important too, keeping in touch with friends, family, ex-colleagues and others to whom we have been referred or introduced. The web links below offer practical, useful advice, much of which is common sense, but it is worth being reminded of.

The final word here will be more directly spiritual. We are loved no less by God because we cannot work. We can encourage those struggling with redundancy to have hope and faith, and we can remember in our prayers all who have been made redundant and are otherwise unemployed. And where unjust structures and employment practices cause suffering to individuals and communities, we commit ourselves to work for justice at every level of society.

Resources

Many of the available online resources are concerned with the financial aspects of redundancy, one example being:

- Citizens Advice Bureau (http://www.citizensadvice.co.uk/en/social-policy/employment-issues/redundancy/)[86] which offers practical advice.

Others offer different types of advice:

- WebMD (http://www.webmd.boots.com/depression/features/depression-and-redundancy-tips)[87] examines the link between redundancy and offers ten useful tips in this regard.
- Totaljobs (http://www.totaljobs.com/careers-advice/unemployment-advice/redundancy-survival-pack)[88] again takes a practical approach to dealing with redundancy and seeking employment.

Scripture

The Christian community loves and serves all

As God's chosen ones, holy and beloved, clothe yourselves with compassion, kindness, humility, meekness, and patience.

86. Accessed 5 December 2013.
87. Accessed 5 December 2013.
88. Accessed 5 December 2013.

> Bear with one another and, if anyone has a complaint against another, forgive each other; just as the Lord has forgiven you, so you also must forgive. Above all, clothe yourselves with love, which binds everything together in perfect harmony.
>
> *Colossians 3:12-14*

Prayer

Lord, help all who have been made redundant,
and all who are looking for work.
Grant them encouragement, hope and belief in their self-worth.
May all the Christian community reach out to those in need,
both in their midst and outside their community.
Through Christ our Lord.
Amen.

Séances

Ed Hone

The popular image

In one of Agatha Christie's earlier novels, *The Sittaford Mystery*, six friends gather round a table for afternoon tea and a game of Bridge. When one of the group confesses he can't play the game, someone else suggests they hold a séance. The lights are dimmed, and before long the table begins to rock, and a message is spelt out: Trevelyan, the local landlord, has been murdered! Sure enough, the message of the departed spirit is proved correct: the murder has indeed taken place. In true Christie style, however, all is not as it seems, and human agents have more to do with the murder than it first appears.

This cameo from a Christie murder-mystery illustrates several common features of séances: intense curiosity regarding life after death, both excitement and fear at the possibility of supernatural engagement, and the constant suspicion that any apparent spiritual presence is merely (conscious or unconscious) human manipulation. This gives a good starting point for Christian pastoral engagement with those who have been involved with, or are toying with the idea of, séances.

Why the séance?

Death is, and always has been, the greatest mystery surrounding human existence: what, if anything, happens to us when we die? Christian teaching about the nature of eternal life is rich, if complex: through the resurrection of Jesus Christ, we inherit the promise of eternal life with God. In the Apostles' Creed we assert belief in the resurrection of the body – the whole person is in God's presence, not just the 'spirit' or 'soul'. In the 'Communion of saints' we enjoy relationship with God and with each other in eternity.

The idea behind séances is quite different: when a person dies, their disembodied spirit may linger, and this spirit may be summoned and communicated with. In some understandings it is the troubled spirit who lingers, trying to complete unfinished business; in others, it is the spirit wishing to reassure or assist a loved one left behind. Traditionally, the séance is held to facilitate communication with the departed: a dimly lit, quiet space is created to minimise distraction, and some means of communication may be employed (a table that can rock, playing cards, Ouija board).

Who might ask for help?

Broadly speaking, people who have been involved in a séance will fall into one of several general categories: the bereaved person, unable to accept fully the loss of their loved one and grasping at spiritual straws; the spiritually curious, wondering if there is truth in the belief that it is possible to be in touch with the spirit world; and those who happen across a séance, perhaps at the invitation of a friend or during some social occasion. The experience of a séance might leave a person entirely unmoved. When, however, a person is disturbed emotionally or spiritually, it is as well that we will be prepared to help.

Pointers

A pastoral approach to séances will necessarily consider in what way the issue is creating a difficulty: what kind of help is being sought? It is possible that someone has been involved in a séance and has been left profoundly disturbed or fearful by the experience; perhaps they are full of remorse for having 'dabbled in the occult' and are afraid of the effect it has had on their relationship with God. In some cases, the person may believe they have been in contact with a spirit, or with evil, and they feel spiritually damaged. Perhaps they are simply confused, not knowing what to think about the whole issue.

The first pastoral necessity is always to listen well to the issue as it is presented; this may seem obvious, but it is vital to determine what problem is actually being presented so that the response may be appropriate and helpful. This listening must be accepting and non-judgemental, to encourage the person to speak freely about their experience. If they feel that they are being judged, they may censor what they say, for fear of criticism. Dismissing séances as dangerous and harmful to spiritual health – or dismissing them as unimportant, even laughable – may not be helpful either. If a person is afraid or disturbed there is no use reinforcing their fear, or ridiculing it.

So the second pastoral pointer is to take seriously what is being said, whilst not over-dramatising the situation. Often the sense of being truly heard is therapeutic in and of itself: the one who has had a frightening, confusing experience finds comfort and reassurance in sharing what they have been through, and having it explained and put into a wider faith context.

Thirdly, we can directly address the spiritual aspect. For Christians, séances are irrelevant to faith. They do not represent what we believe about life and about life after death. They can indeed be harmful where they impede the natural grieving process, keeping those who are bereaved locked in to a denial of the death of a loved one. There can be a tendency to morbidity in the refusal to let go of someone who is loved and lost. Our best response here is to offer in other ways the support and comfort of which the bereaved may be in need. Also, as in any pastoral situation, the pastoral carer needs to acknowledge when they are out of their depth, and to refer their client to a counsellor or other appropriately qualified person.

In answer to the stereotypical séance question, 'Is there anybody there?' the Christian answers, 'I am here, and God is here, and in God you will find new and everlasting life.'

Scripture

The Christian is preoccupied not with death, but with life

> To another he said, 'Follow me.' But he said, 'Lord, first let me go and bury my father.' But Jesus said to him, 'Let the dead bury their own dead; but as for you, go and proclaim the kingdom of God.'
>
> *Luke 9:59, 60*

Prayer

Lord Jesus,
breathe your Holy Spirit of life into us that we may truly live.
As you died and rose again,
you call us to new life in you.
Help us to follow that call with all our heart,
and announce it to all whom we meet.
Amen.

Sterilisation

John Parr

Story

Joe and Emma are in their early thirties and have been together for ten years. Throughout their relationship they have made real efforts to adopt what they see as a responsible lifestyle: watching the amount of energy they use, buying fairly traded goods whenever possible and more recently growing some of their own food. They don't see themselves as preachy paragons of virtue who are out to save the planet, but they do think that 'everyone should do their bit'.

Before Joe and Emma had children, they felt that two would be enough. Their third is now 18 months old. She was a 'surprise', and they soon learned to welcome her. But they believe a fourth would be irresponsible. They can point to all the relevant facts and figures about how much of the Earth's resources relatively prosperous families like theirs are likely to use across their lifetime. At present they can just about squeeze into their house, which is not far from the town centre. They don't particularly want to move to a bigger house further out of town because they would have to use their car more often, and they have recently had to buy a bigger one for safety reasons. Time is one of their most precious resources, and with increasingly busy lives they know that there are limits as to how far it will stretch. They want to be able to give their children as much time as they need, and they feel this would be compromised if their family grew any bigger.

Emma has been taking the contraceptive pill for nearly 15 years, and she does not relish the prospect of continuing until the menopause. She and Joe both want a form of contraception that is as near to 100 per cent reliable as possible. They believe that the simplest option would be for Joe to have a vasectomy. They know several couples of their age who have gone down this route, with no adverse effects. The only difference they speak of is that they no longer have to worry about contraception or having any more children. Joe and Emma are almost convinced, but they wonder about the 'what ifs'. Two couples in their circle of friends have recently split up. And last year the six-year-old son of Emma's sister died in a road accident.

As well as discussing their concerns with Joe's GP, they decide to talk to their pastor, especially after reading some challenging material on websites from the more conservative end of the Christian spectrum.

Forms of sterilisation

Sterilisation refers to a range of surgical procedures that make a woman or a man incapable of reproduction. Some of these interventions are carried out for medical reasons while others are forms of contraception. Sterilisation is also one of the surgical procedures involved in gender reassignment (sex change).

For women, the most common form of sterilisation involves removing, blocking or cutting the fallopian tubes which carry eggs from the ovaries to the womb (tubal ligation). As a result, eggs and sperm do not meet, thus preventing fertilisation, and the eggs are reabsorbed by the woman's body. A more radical form of female sterilisation involves removing the uterus (hysterectomy), but this is not usually carried out for sterilisation alone. In most cases tubal ligation is a relatively minor operation, usually carried out under general anaesthetic and causing short-lived discomfort. It is, however, very difficult to reverse, and should therefore only be considered as a form of contraception by those who do not wish to have children, or any more children. Most sterilisations are carried out on women who are over 30, and it has become increasingly popular in the UK since the late 1960s. In 2009–10 more than 10,000 women were sterilised. The operation is more than 99 per cent effective, though the failure rate is higher for women under 28. Long-term adverse effects are rare, though sterilisation does bring an increased risk of ectopic pregnancy. It has no effect on a woman's sex drive or hormone levels.

Vasectomy is the most common form of male sterilisation and involves cutting, blocking or sealing the tubes (vas deferens) that carry sperm from the testicles to the penis. The operation is usually carried out under local anaesthetic and is brief and relatively painless. It is almost 100 per cent effective, though in a very small number of cases the vas deferens has been known to heal. Following a vasectomy the body continues to produce sperm, but as they are no longer able to travel along the vas deferens, they are reabsorbed by the body. Vasectomy is currently chosen by an estimated 13 per cent of men in the UK. In some cases it can be reversed, but there is no guarantee of success. There are no serious long-term health risks, though a very small number of men experience chronic testicular pain, for which treatment is often unsuccessful. There is no firm evidence linking vasectomy to prostate or testicular cancer (although regular health screening is advised).

The consent of a partner (assuming one exists) is not required either for male or female sterilisation, but those considering it are advised to discuss it with a doctor, nurse or counsellor.

Alternatives to female sterilisation take the form of long-acting contraception. A contraceptive implant inserted into the upper arm releases the hormone progestogen, which stops the release of an egg from the ovary, thickens the mucus in the cervix and thins the lining of the womb. As a result it is more difficult for the sperm to travel through the cervix and for the womb to support a fertilised egg. The implant lasts for three years and is almost 100 per cent effective. An intra-muscular contraceptive injection of progestogen is given every 8 to 12 weeks and is more than 99 per cent effective. An intra-uterine device can be inserted in the womb for between five and ten years, though it can be removed sooner. Some of these release progestogen, while others prevent fertilisation or implantation of the fertilised egg in the wall of the uterus. Again, these devices are more than 99 per cent effective.

Attitudes towards sterilisation

There are misgivings about sterilisation. Compulsory sterilisation has been used during the twentieth century in a number of countries – including Canada, USA, Peru, India, China, Japan and Sweden – as a form of birth control, to prevent the spread of hereditary conditions and reduce the population of minorities. In Puerto Rico, a government-backed programme brought about the compulsory sterilisation of one-third of its women by 1965. The International Criminal Court regards compulsory sterilisation as a crime against humanity when it is part of a widespread or systematic action by a government.

Religions offer a wide range of attitudes towards contraception and sterilisation, with objections coming from those who insist on the connections between sexual intercourse, procreation and divine blessing.[89] Within Christianity, the official Roman Catholic position is that any human intervention that interferes with procreation is against natural law and the teaching of the Bible.[90] However, some Catholics who uphold the Church's traditional teaching are prepared to countenance sterilisation as an alternative to abortion in the case of a woman whose learning disability makes it impossible for her to consent to sexual intercourse.[91] Orthodox Christianity contains a wide spectrum of opinion.[92] Protestants tend not to

89. See http://contraception.about.com/od/additionalresources/ss/religion.htm (accessed 23 November 2013).

90. Pope Paul VI's encyclical *Humanae Vitae* (1968) reaffirmed traditional Roman Catholic teaching, and has been followed by successive Popes.

91. See www.twotlj.org/G-3-54.html (accessed 23 November 2013).

92. See John Meyendorff (1975), *Marriage: An Orthodox Perspective*, Crestwood: St Vladimir's Seminary Press.

oppose voluntary sterilisation, though some conservative evangelicals appeal to the objections of sixteenth-century Reformers to contraception to justify their stance.[93]

Pastoral wisdom

The wise pastor will want to know whether the proposed sterilisation is voluntary. If a woman for whom it is being considered cannot give consent, then it is essential that those who are responsible for making the decision are confident that sterilisation is clearly in her best interest. Specialist forms of advocacy may be available to support those whose capacity to make medical decisions is impaired.

Whether voluntary sterilisation is considered appropriate depends on its purpose. Some religious people will see all forms of sterilisation that are not carried out solely to benefit a woman's health as instances of 'playing God'. A more moderate approach will want to balance the general effectiveness and lack of side effects of sterilisation against its nature as a radical intervention. As an example of our ability to remake human bodies in our own image, sterilisation may be seen as an act of faithful and responsible living. According to St Paul's injunction to 'present your bodies as a living sacrifice, holy and acceptable to God' (Romans 12:1), our experience of God's salvation is always embodied. In the absence of direct guidance on sterilisation (as with many issues of contemporary concern), Christians will want to ask whether they can envisage voluntary sterilisation as an example of embodied worship.

As a lifestyle choice that allows worry-free contraception, the rightness of sterilisation may of course be called into question by the subsequent death of one's child, or the breakdown of a relationship and the desire to have a child with another partner. Many are prepared to act in good faith, live in hope and take the risk, or pay the price of further surgery should this become desirable or possible.

Further help

- Family Planning Association: www.fpa.org.uk[94]
- National Health Service: www.nhs.uk/conditions and follow the links[95]

93. See Charles D. Provan (1989), *The Bible and Birth Control*, Monongahela, PA: Zimmer Printing. The relevant chapter is available at www.jesus-passion.com/contraception.htm (accessed 23 November 2013).
94. Accessed 23 November 2013.
95. Accessed 23 November 2013.

- Brook Advisory Service: www.brook.org.uk[96]
- Marie Stopes International: www.mariestopes.org.uk[97]

Prayer

Loving and tender God,
you have made us in your image
and call us to honour you
in body, mind and spirit.
Give us courage and wisdom
that we may be
honest in what we desire,
faithful in what we intend,
open to what we have not yet considered
and humble in all that we do,
for the sake of Jesus Christ our Lord.
Amen.

96. Accessed 23 November 2013.
97. Accessed 23 November 2013.

Troubled by spirits

John Cox

Story

The cook in the church school kitchen was worried about Bridget, one of her staff, a young Afro-Caribbean mum. Bridget had only recently come to the school and seemed to be very anxious. On more than one occasion she had been found crying. The cook looked for an opportunity to ask her whether there was any problem, wondering if she was finding the work too much or was feeling homesick.

Bridget was reluctant at first to explain the situation, although she was obviously troubled. But bit by bit it all came out. She and her husband were convinced that the house they were living in was haunted. 'We hear things,' she explained, 'and there's a cold feeling in our bedroom. I'm sure it's an evil spirit.' The cook was too wise to simply dismiss Bridget's fears. It wasn't the first time she had come across the problem. But she didn't feel she was the person to help. Knowing that Bridget attended the local church she suggested she went to see the vicar. Bridget did so and he arranged to visit Bridget and her husband in their home.

When Bridget went to work next day she seemed much more at ease, as though a burden had been lifted from her. She would say little about it, just that the vicar had talked with them and prayed with them and then said a prayer in each room of the house and the bad spirit wasn't there any more. She and her husband were much happier.

The situation

Belief in evil spirits and ghosts is more prevalent in some cultures than others, but it can potentially appear wherever there is faith in the 'spiritual'. Some people appear to be especially sensitive and aware of the presence of 'spirits', and aspects of the paranormal make a regular appearance in the tabloid newspapers as well as more serious journals. Common experiences are of unexplained cold areas in a room, noises as though someone were walking about, objects being moved for no apparent reason. Houses acquire a reputation of being haunted, and hotels sometimes even advertise bedrooms where a ghost has been seen. People test their bravery, or their scepticism, by booking such a room.

Rationalists and secularists understandably scorn the 'spiritual' explanations and look for more rational causations. 'Ghost hunters' may make good children's stories or gothic novels but have comparatively little everyday credence among many people in the modern world.

By the very nature of the subject, it is difficult to obtain an 'objective' view. People of faith will themselves vary, from those who treat the whole topic of spirit beings, ghosts, etc. with immense caution to those who readily believe in at least some aspects. Spiritualists are certainly not confined to the annals of Victorian flummery, and many people would claim that they receive help from the messages conveyed through a spirit medium. A Gallup survey in the United States in 2005 indicated that 37 per cent of the people polled believed in haunted houses, 32 per cent in ghosts, 21 per cent in witches.[98] Other surveys have shown that 70 per cent of people believe they have experienced some kind of paranormal event.

Being 'troubled by spirits' conveys a wide range of experience, and generalisations should be viewed with caution. Although troubled by them, some people are not particularly frightened or threatened by the 'spirits'. They are viewed more of a nuisance than anything else. Those seeking a rational approach suggest that the experience might be more simply explained through misunderstanding, misperception or misinterpretation of 'odd' but natural occurrences. For some people it is their own internal problems, or tensions in relationships with others – perhaps a husband or wife – that become unconsciously projected out into the 'spirit'. In this way the spirit becomes the manifestation of psychological or relational problems.

At the extreme pole from this position are those who believe themselves or others to be 'possessed' by demons, or indeed by the devil. It has been traditionally understood that in this situation the help of an exorcist is required. Cases of criminal activity arising from belief in demon possession appear occasionally in the media, most tragically when this involves the murder of children believed by their relatives to have been possessed. Such events indicate the extreme danger of this belief. Nevertheless, the Church has always recognised the possibility of 'possession', and both Anglican and Roman Catholic dioceses have priests authorised by the bishop to deal with reported cases of 'possession'. Even in these circumstances, great care is first taken to exclude other possible reasons, such as

98. http://www.gallup.com/poll/17275/OneThird-Americans-Believe-Dearly-May-Departed.aspx (accessed 8 December 2013).

psychological disturbance, projection or a medical condition. Where an exorcism is carried out, only liturgical or ritual forms that have been authorised may be used, and care is taken neither to sensationalise nor publicise the event.

The pastoral response

Dealing with the paranormal at whatever level requires both care and skill. In the case where it is believed that 'exorcism' is in some way required, only authorised people should handle it. The pastor should not hesitate in making a referral to the appropriate person.

But not every troubled person believes they are possessed. The normal skills of pastoral care will come into play, i.e. listening, discerning what may be the underlying issues and deciding on the most effective way forward, with the interests of the person paramount. Pastors should be careful not to jump to hasty conclusions, being neither gullible nor overly sceptical. Awareness of psychological factors may well lead to a referral to a suitably qualified counsellor – with the person's permission, of course.

The pastor may be able to offer effective help. Listening and talking will be involved but, as in the case of the story above, prayer and action may also be very appropriate – prayer of comfort and reassurance, and action (such as going into every room in the house and saying prayers) that is believed by both the pastor and the person to be relevant and acceptable. So, for example, if the person said that cutting the neck of a chicken and sprinkling its blood throughout the house was the only acceptable effective action, a Christian pastor may well understand the cultural nuances but feel unable to carry out such an act. Such differences of viewpoint would be discussed. Ultimately the aim is to help the person feel 'at ease' in themselves and with others. It may take time to achieve. Christian prayer draws upon the power and love of God for that person.

Resources

There are many websites offering help in matters involving the paranormal, e.g. ghost hunting. Sensible caution is required in making use of them. Some are harmless to the extent that they recognise that what they are doing is more in the realm of leisure enjoyment and fantasy than serious counselling. But some make questionable claims to be 'scientific'.

For Roman Catholics and Anglicans, the best approach is to contact the bishop's office for advice.

Scripture

In Jesus' time there was a clear understanding, at least among some of the Jews, that people could be troubled or possessed by spirits and demons. When accused by the Pharisees of casting out demons by Beelzebub the prince of demons, Jesus asked them, 'by whom do your exorcists cast them out?' (Luke 11:19). The issue was one of authority and by whose power such exorcisms could be carried out, not a dispute about the reality of possession. Jesus himself cast out unclean spirits (Mark 1:21-8) and he gave his disciples the authority to do the same (Mark 6:6, 7). Even those who were not directly following Jesus appear to have cast out demons in his name (Mark 9:38-40). St Paul, too, is reported to have performed such acts in the name of Christ (Acts 19:11-13). This understanding of the spirit world and how in the name of God or Christ the unclean (evil) spirits could be dealt with persisted. Not only was it a sign of people following in the way of Christ's own mission of care for those in distress but it was also a sign of the ongoing struggle between 'good' and 'evil'.

Prayers

The following prayers are taken from the Church of England website.

May the Lord hear you in the day of trouble,
the name of the God of Jacob defend you;
send you help from his sanctuary
and strengthen you out of Zion;
remember all your offerings
and accept your burnt sacrifice;
grant you your heart's desire
and fulfil all your mind.
Amen. *Psalm 20:1-4*

O Lord Jesus Christ,
present with us now in his risen power,
enter into your body and spirit,
take from you all that harms and hinders you,
and fill you with his healing and his peace.
Amen.

Christ be with you: Christ within you;
Christ before you: Christ behind you;
Christ on your right: Christ on your left;
Christ above you: Christ beneath you;
Christ around you: now and ever.

Bind unto yourself the name,
the strong name of the Trinity;
by invocation of the same,
the Three in One and One in Three.
Of whom all nature hath creation,
Eternal Father, Spirit, Word:
praise the Lord of your salvation,
salvation is of Christ the Lord.

Almighty God, heavenly Father,
breathe your Holy Spirit into the heart of this your servant *N*
and inspire *him/her* with love for goodness and truth.
May *he/she*, fearing only you, have no other fear;
knowing your compassion, be ever mindful of your love;
and serving you faithfully unto death, live eternally with you,
through Jesus Christ our Lord.
Amen.

Victims

John Parr

Story

The signing of the Armistice in 1918 brought hope and excitement to Ethel. Her fiancé Frank had been conscripted in 1916 and she hadn't seen him for more than two years. 'It won't be long now before he's home,' she thought, 'and then we'll be able to make plans for our wedding and our future together.'

When Frank finally arrived home early in 1919, Ethel soon realised that although he had survived the war without injury, he was not unscathed by his experience. For most of his time in Germany he had been a prisoner of war after his unit surrendered. After the war ended, he and his fellow prisoners were released without food or shelter. Many of them died of exhaustion and never made it home. Frank and his unit travelled through France and were met by cavalry, who put them on lorries that took them to a reception centre. From there they went to Calais, and then to Dover and home.

However much Ethel tried to get Frank to talk about what he'd been through, he was reluctant to let her into his world. In fact, he hardly talked about his life as a soldier to anyone. The most he shared with her was the message he'd received from King George V, which included these words: 'We are thankful that this longed for day has arrived, and that back in the old Country you will be able once more to enjoy the happiness of a home and to see good days among those who anxiously look for your return'.

Ethel's hopes for the happiness of a home with Frank were dashed in June 1919 when he broke off their engagement. She was so shocked that she couldn't speak. She lived with her mother and father and brother, and they had to break the news to family and friends, and to her employers in a local office. Ethel withdrew from the world and hardly emerged from her bedroom. She ate very little and noticeably lost weight. After a month her family called in the doctor, who recognised the signs of shock and encouraged them to believe that she'd get over it once the better weather arrived.

That proved to be wishful thinking. Ethel remained a prisoner of her trauma. By the end of the year she had been admitted to an asylum seven miles away, where she spent the rest of her life, talking only to herself.

The nature of victimisation

A victim is someone who suffers injury or deprivation as a result of the actions of others. Victimisation comes in many forms. A person may be the victim of an accident, a natural disaster, a downturn in the economy, an illness, an abusive relationship, a violent crime, a war, an oppressive political system.

Bullying is one of the most common types of victimisation. It occurs wherever people come into contact with each other, including on social networking media, and involves physical harm, threats and verbal abuse such as name-calling, gossip and slander. It is motivated by jealousy, resentment or the desire to conceal shame, anxiety or low self-esteem. Victims of bullying are often chosen because they are different from others, perhaps in their physical characteristics, social background or sexual orientation. Their experiences often result in mental ill-health, low self-esteem, increased susceptibility to illness, social isolation and even suicide. According to a survey carried out in 2006, 69 per cent of children in the UK report being bullied.[99] A report published by the Samaritans organisation in 2008 claimed that 80 per cent of employees in the UK are affected by bullying in the workplace, resulting in the loss of 19 million working days annually, at a cost of £13 billion.[100]

Another form of victimisation is *scapegoating*, which involves using exceptional individual behaviour or the way a minority acts to characterise the whole person or group. People who are mentally ill or physically disabled, the Traveller community and those who claim welfare benefits can find themselves victimised in this way. Scapegoating is often a defence mechanism, as in the case of a whistle-blower in a workplace who is ostracised or even sacked because he or she exposes the shortcomings of colleagues or managers.

Victimhood is no respecter of persons, though some appear to be more vulnerable than others to the experience. For example, the risk of violent victimisation is unevenly spread. Studies show that among homeless people this is greater among women, those who have serious mental health problems or abuse drugs or alcohol. A British study shows that 16 per cent of people with established psychotic disorders living in the wider community in London reported violent victimisation (according to the British Crime Survey, comparable figures for London as a whole were 6.7 per cent).[101] Similar results have been found elsewhere in the world.

---

99. For statistical information on children's experience of bullying see http://www.beatbullying.org/dox/resources/statistics.html (accessed 24 November 2013).
100. See http://www.bullyingbusiness.co.uk (accessed 24 November 2013).
101. See Elizabeth Walsh, Paul Moran et al, 'Prevalence of violent victimisation in severe mental illness', *The British Journal of Psychiatry* (2003) 183: 233-238.

Among commuters travelling on London buses, people under 18 are at a disproportionately high risk of experiencing robbery, physical and sexual violence.[102]

Victims inhabit a complex world. Some victims experience *secondary victimisation*. An asylum seeker fled to the UK from his home country because his father was murdered. Though he was granted asylum, his distressing experiences resulted in mental illness, with the additional victimisation this is known to bring. Victims of rape tell of not being believed by police and other agencies, and even of being dissuaded from pursuing charges. In some societies they are disowned by family and friends.

Some victims are statistically more likely to experience *re-victimisation*. Among them are those who experience sexual abuse and people who are burgled.[103] The theory of 'learned helplessness' is one way of explaining the processes involved in re-victimisation.[104] Some tend to see themselves as victims whether or not what happens to them can be blamed entirely on others, and they may be unwilling or unable to take their share of responsibility for their situation. Such *self-victimisation* may be a coping strategy or a means of gaining attention. Some who habitually feel victimised can turn those who try to help them into victims when they prove not to be the hoped-for rescuer.

Victims of discrimination now have legal protection in many parts of the world. In the UK the Equality Act 2010 sets out nine 'protected characteristics' on which it is unlawful to discriminate: age, disability, gender, gender reassignment, marriage and civil partnership, pregnancy or maternity, race, religion and belief, and sexual orientation. This law also protects the children and siblings of those who complain about victimisation. For example, if parents complain that their daughter was not allowed to take part in a school metalwork class, the school is not allowed to victimise the pupil or her siblings as a result of the complaint.

102. The Jill Dando Institute of Security and Crime Science at University College, London was established in 1991, two years after she was murdered at the entrance to her home. The Institute's research into repeat and public transport victimisation is available on its website http://www.ucl.ac.uk/jdi (accessed 24 November 2013).

103. According to the 1996 International Crime Survey, more than 40 per cent of sexual offences and physical assaults (actual or threatened), 28 per cent of robberies and 17 per cent of burglaries, are repeats. In the case of burglary it is thought that returning offenders are keen to maximise benefit as well as minimise risk and search time.

104. See Martin E. P. Seligman (1975), *Helplessness: On Depression, Development, and Death,* San Francisco: W. H. Freeman.

Victims in the Bible

Concern for victims runs through the Bible. Joseph – victim of his father's indulgence and his brothers' consequent jealousy – puts his position in Pharaoh's administration to good use by helping his family when they fall victim to famine (Genesis 37–45). His descendants become victims of a later Pharaoh's oppression (Exodus 1:8-22). When they are eventually liberated, the law given to their leader, Moses, shows support for victims of illness, poverty, debt and injustice. The prophets of Israel regularly speak up for victims of greed on the part of the wealthy.

The general context of Jesus' ministry was one in which his own people had become victims of imperial expansion. They lived under the authority of a distant power, present through its occupying army. Some Jews were victims of the way powerful groups had responded to this, notably those whose zeal to preserve a distinctive identity for their people led them to victimise those who were unable or unwilling to conform. Much of Jesus' ministry sees him in the company of particular victims. His attitude is informed by his interpretation of the will of God according to the weightier matters of the law, among them justice, mercy and faith (Matthew 23:23). The Gospels depict Jesus among people who are deprived of these virtues and values, while his response is to embody them. In one of his most memorable stories, a Samaritan crosses racial boundaries to care for a Jewish victim of violence, at some risk and cost to himself (Luke10:30-37). Jesus' parable of the last judgement (Matthew 25:31-46) has the agent of God's reign, the Son of Man, highlighting the eternal significance of showing solidarity with victims of hunger, injustice and isolation. In the end, Jesus himself becomes a victim of political expediency and the violence used by the ruling elites to control and subdue his people.

Help

The wise pastor, seeking to support those who are victims, will be informed by Jesus' identification with victims of many kinds. His example and teaching, together with the way these have inspired his followers in widely different circumstances, encourage us towards greater understanding of what makes and keeps people victims, and how best to respond to their plight in the spirit of justice, mercy and love. Pastoral care involves directing victims to specialist sources of help when necessary, particularly those that provide information, legal advice or advocacy. These include:

- Citizens Advice: www.citizensadvice.org.uk[105]
- Samaritans: www.samaritans.org[106]
- Workplace bullying: www.bullyingbusiness.co.uk[107]
- Bullying: www.beatbullying.org[108]
- Crime: www.victimsupport.org.uk[109]

Prayer

Lord Jesus Christ,
whose cry of abandonment from the cross
shows your solidarity with all who are victimised
through misunderstanding, rejection or violence,
comfort us when we suffer through the actions of others,
strengthen us when we are tempted to withdraw from the agony of others,
and forgive us when we are the reason for the pain of others.
Amen.

105. Accessed 24 November 2013.
106. Accessed 24 November 2013.
107. Accessed 24 November 2013.
108. Accessed 24 November 2013.
109. Accessed 24 November 2013.

Violent death

Paul Cox

Story

Anthony was a successful, high-flying young accountant who had audited books for large companies at home and abroad. He had had reservations about the business activity of one of his clients and had raised the issue with the CEO. Early one morning, as he was getting dressed ready to leave for work, he was abducted and later murdered. His body was never found. Those directly responsible, having fled abroad, were not brought to court, although they were held in prison for some time. It turned out to be a very complicated case for the police. For Sarah, his partner, it was devastating. The funeral was held only after a considerable delay. The local community was as supportive as it could be.

Jane was the eldest of three daughters of the local school's head teacher. On a dark, wet November evening, driving home from Heathrow, she was hit by another car. She died at the scene of the crash. The other driver was hardly injured. Jane's father felt his life was shattered. At the court hearing he pleaded that the court should take no further action against the offending driver. He felt he had to forgive the young man. Although the father continued in his career for another five years, he was never the same brilliant head teacher that his former pupils had known him to be.

Statistics

In 2010/11, the UK police provisionally recorded 642 offences of murder. There has been a general downward trend in police-recorded murders over recent years. The number of attempted murders recorded by the police in 2010/11 was 525, an 11 per cent decrease compared with the previous year.

Department of Transport statistics show that in 2011 there were 1850 road deaths. This was the first time the annual figure had increased since 2003.

By late September 2012 the death toll for British personnel in Afghanistan since operations began in 2002 had reached 433.

Attitudes – a moral dilemma

Of the people directly involved in these statistics, only the military dead have been nationally named and recorded by the media.

Wootton Bassett has been given the title of 'Royal' in recognition of its show of respect and honour to the military personnel who have been killed and brought back to Britain by air transport. Yet for Jane's and Anthony's families the loss is no less. The possibility of their deaths was not anticipated, as it may well be for the families of men and women serving in the armed forces. The military make the choice to serve their country, knowing that it may mean death. An accountant and a young graduate did not have any choice about the situations that were fatal for them. A dog kills a child and there is an immediate reaction that makes keeping that particular breed illegal. But we are tolerant of the number of road deaths each year. We do not ban motor vehicles, and even punish relatively lightly those who cause fatal accidents.

Pastoral care

Reactions, both public and private, to violent death vary considerably. Honouring, public recognition, demands for severe punishment (including capital punishment), anger, devastation, bewilderment and forgiveness have all been expressed in response to violent death. The questioning that reflects the moral dilemma outlined above may be delayed but still can be acutely felt and expressed.

In pastoral care it is essential to be aware of the stages of grief and bereavement so that appropriate help can be given, not just immediately but over a longer time period, even over years.[110] The funeral service may be the time when the shortened life is celebrated and acknowledged for its worth. This is what the military are used to in their particular expression of funeral rites. It was also seen in Manchester at the funerals of the two policewomen who were murdered in September 2012.

In cases of road death, and especially in cases of murder, police family liaison officers are trained to work with the close families of victims. Not only do they give support but they also keep the family informed about the actions that are being taken by the police to find and convict the murderer. In a case such as Anthony's there is the added trauma of not knowing what actually happened. There is the devastating moment when the police say that the incident is to be treated as murder, even without the evidence of a body. (This occurred after four days in the case of the abduction and assumed murder of April Jones in Machynlleth in October 2012.)

110. A helpful book is Colin Murray Parkes & Holly G Prigerson, *Bereavement: Studies in Adult Life* (fourth edition) (Penguin, 2010).

Then there is no coffin, only a service of thanksgiving for the life so tragically taken. The moment for closure is not clear, any more than it was for all the families who heard that their loved one was missing in action, presumed dead.

Violent death makes us all feel just that bit more vulnerable. It is a violation of the human spirit, as well as of the body. Comforting words seem so inadequate. For adults this is bad enough, but what of children who have lost their parent(s)? The words for them depend so much upon their age. The details of the deaths need only be told if they are old enough to understand and to cope, and even then in terms that are appropriate to their emotional as well as their chronological age.

Violent death leaves its own particular scars on loved ones, scars that may in time be covered up but seldom vanish. Specialist help may well be needed if the effects change the circumstances of those affected, such as inability to continue work for a period of time. In a case of three orphaned children, the village community, encouraged by the local church congregation, raised funds to provide for them, enabling the care to be more personal than social services alone could provide.

Other help

There are some helpful books that provide shared experiences, although not all are necessarily about violent deaths.

- *'You'll Get Over it': the Rage of Bereavement* by Virginia Ironside (Penguin, 1997)
- *On Grief and Grieving: Finding the Meaning of Grief Through the Five Stages of Loss* by Elizabeth Kübler-Ross and David Kessler (Simon & Schuster, 2005)

Cruse is an organisation that provides support for the bereaved, including published guidance on supporting young people.
Website: http://www.cruse.org.uk/[111]
Telephone 0844 477 9400
Email helpline@cruse.org.uk

111. Accessed 5 December 2013.

Prayer

Lord God, almighty Father,
as your Son, Jesus Christ, suffered a violent death,
be with us in our grief,
calm us in our anger,
bring peace to us in the face of violence,
and may we remember with thanks the life of N
so suddenly ended, with no word of goodbye.
Amen.